ACCLAIM FOR TODD WILBUR'S
TOP SECRET RECIPES SERIES

"There's something almost magically compelling
about the idea of making such foods at home ... The
allure is undeniable, and [the books are] stuffed with tidbits and
lore you're unlikely to find anywhere else."
—*Boston Herald*

"The mission: Decode the secret recipes for America's
favorite junk foods. Equipment: Standard kitchen appliances.
Goal: Leak the results to a ravenous public."
—*USA Today*

"This is the cookbook to satisfy all your cravings."
—Juli Huss, author of *The Faux Gourmet*

TODD WILBUR is the author of *Top Secret Recipes, More Top Secret Recipes, Top Secret Restaurant Recipes, Top Secret Recipes Lite!,*
and *Low-Fat Top Secret Recipes* (all available from Plume). When
not taste-testing recipes on himself, his friends, or TV talk-show
hosts, Todd lives in Las Vegas.

TOP SECRET RECIPES

SODAS, SMOOTHIES, SPIRITS, & SHAKES

Creating Cool Kitchen Clones of America's Favorite Brand-Name Drinks

TODD WILBUR

Illustrated by the Author

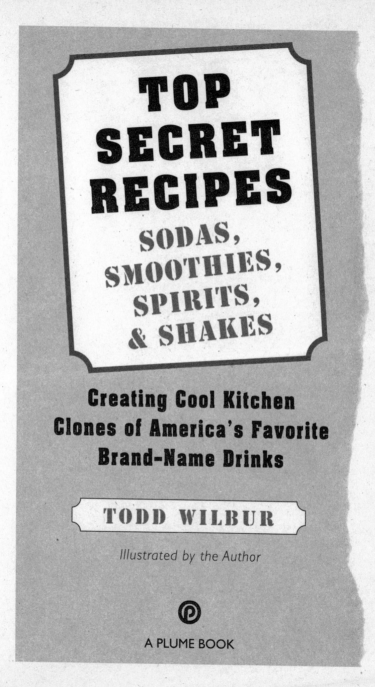

A PLUME BOOK

PLUME
Published by the Penguin Group
Penguin Putnam Inc., 375 Hudson Street,
New York, New York 10014, U.S.A.
Penguin Books Ltd, 80 Strand,
London WC2R 0RL England
Penguin Books Australia Ltd, Ringwood,
Victoria, Australia
Penguin Books Canada Ltd, 10 Alcorn Avenue,
Toronto, Ontario, Canada M4V 3B2
Penguin Books (N.Z.) Ltd, 182–190 Wairau Road,
Auckland 10, New Zealand

Penguin Books Ltd, Registered Offices:
Harmondsworth, Middlesex, England

First published by Plume, a member of Penguin Putnam Inc.

First Printing, February 2002
10 9 8 7 6 5 4 3 2

To the best of the author's knowledge, the information regarding company backgrounds and product histories is true and accurate. Any misrepresentation of factual material is completely unintentional.

Ⓟ REGISTERED TRADEMARK—MARCA REGISTRADA

CIP data is available.
ISBN 0-452-28318-3

Printed in the United States of America
Set in Gill Sans Light

For Pamela —
she's the real thing.
Beautiful inside and out.
She's my proof that
soul mates do exist.

CONTENTS

SHAKES

SPIRITS
SCHNAPPS & LIQUEURS

SPIRITS
COCKTAILS

SPIRITS
MIXERS

INTRODUCTION

Today I've been drinking the world's number one beverage but I can't give you the recipe. Unless you already know how to combine two hydrogen atoms with one oxygen atom in abundance, you'll have to settle for drinking it out of a bottle or straight off the tap.

What I can give you, though, is a bunch of recipes to duplicate the taste of the other drinks we hold dear, including several iced versions for the second most popular beverage in the world: tea. You'll recognize many of these products, because it would be nearly impossible to exist in civilization on this planet without being reminded several times each day that you absolutely must drink these wonderful drinks. And that you will enjoy them. And that when you are thirsty again you will come back for more.

It's true that this book includes clone recipes for some of the most successful products in the world—those drinks you've enjoyed since birth—with long, remarkable histories and huge profits. But a collection such as this would not be complete without also including copycat formulas for the newer, trendier drinks that have garnered more recent worship.

Sure, I've got recipes in here for sodas, milk shakes, smoothies, lemonades, coffee drinks, and punches, but this book isn't just for the teetotalers. If you, uh, "total" more than "tee," I've got some of the coolest cocktail, mixer and liqueur-making recipes ever assembled. Spirits were around a long time before fizzy flavored sodas and grande Frappuccinos, and this book recognizes that delicious cocktail recipes are just as fun to re-create at home as are recipes for famous foodstuffs found in previous *Top Secret Recipes* volumes.

This book is divided into two major sections, with the first half consisting of clone recipes for famous sodas, milk shakes, and smoothies, plus a section for drinks that don't fit into those three categories. This is where you learn how to re-create your favorite sodas using the old soda fountain technique: adding flavored syrup to cold soda water. This is also where you get the secret to mixing a Dairy Queen Blizzard clone of your own at home so that the ice cream won't get too runny when you stir in all the chunks. If you like coffee, you'll find out what secret ingredients will copy a Starbucks Frappuccino and the instant General Foods International Coffees. You'll find out how to make the perfect lemonade from scratch and how to duplicate the taste of Sunny Delight using more fruit juice than the real thing's got in it.

The second half of the book is devoted to spirits. This is where you find clone recipes for famous brands such as Kahlúa, Bailey's Irish Cream, and Grand Marnier. You'll find out how to add flavorings and fruit to inexpensive vodka to create a variety of delicious liqueurs. In this section you'll also get dozens and dozens of recipes for the most popular cocktails from America's largest restaurant chains. If you've ever been to Applebee's, Chili's, T.G.I. Friday's, Planet Hollywood, or Outback Steakhouse and have seen the glossy table cards with beautiful photos of delicious and colorful cocktails on them and wished you could make drinks that good at home, this is where you learn how. And right at the end you'll get the secrets to making the delicious mixers that go into those awesome drinks, all from scratch.

So grab a straw and dive on in. As with all the other *Top Secret Recipes* books, measure carefully and follow the directions precisely. In no time at all you'll soon be downing a duplicate of your favorite drink, from your favorite glass, while sitting in your favorite chair.

If you'd like to try some clone recipes for solid food, check out the other books in the *Top Secret Recipes* series or come to the web site at www.TopSecretRecipes.com.

If you have suggestions for other drinks to clone, drop me some e-mail at Todd@topsecretrecipes.com.

I'll be back again to uncover more of your most requested clone cuisine secrets in the next book, *Even More Top Secret Recipes*, coming soon. Until then, cheers to you.

—Todd Wilbur

SODAS

When America figured out how to mix carbon dioxide gas with water in the early 1800s a monumental industry was born. The fizzy fluid, invented to clone carbonated water found in natural springs, was originally thought to be a magical curative for a variety of ailments ranging from indigestion to arthritis. Ambitious pharmacists looking to strike it rich with their own new "patent medicines" added custom mixtures of herbs, flowers, fruits, berries, and bark to the soda water, creating a wide range of flavors with a variety of claimed health benefits. Their background in medicine and chemistry made these pharmacists perfectly suited for such a task, despite the many dubious claims of miracle cures provided by the new formulas. It is these pharmacists who are responsible for launching today's monumental soft drink industry.

Since alcoholic drinks are called "hard drinks," the new beverages became "soft drinks." But they were more than just bubbling thirst quenchers, since soft drinks in this era had some potent medicinal ingredients: Coca-Cola contained cocaine extracted from coca leaves to provide energy; Pespi-Cola contained pepsin, an enzyme to aid in digestion; and 7UP came packed with lithium, used today to treat depression and mental illness.

Through the end of the 1800s and into the twentieth century, customers stopped in at soda fountains at their local pharmacies for a dose of chat, refreshment, and remedy, and walked out with a great big smile. It's no wonder these stores became the central attraction in town. At the soda fountain, when a soft drink was ordered, sweetened syrup was added to cold soda water, it was stirred up a bit and served ready to drink. In the early days of these soda fountains ice cream sodas were hugely popular, as were root beer, ginger ale, and a whole mess of different cola drinks.

Still, the soda business was limited by the fact that customers needed access to a pharmacy. For soda pioneers to make their products fly high they had to figure out how to go from getting the people to the soda, to getting the soda to the people. At first, glass bottles blown by hand were filled with the drink and capped with corks. But pressure from the carbonation was too much for the early stoppers, and many bottles blew their tops before arriving at their destinations. Inventors racked their brains for years to figure out a design for the perfect stopper until, 1500 patents later, the crown bottle cap was invented in 1892. The glass bottle–blowing machine followed the crown cap a few years after that, and the soda distribution industry popped into high gear.

When Prohibition made it illegal to drink the hard stuff, soda sales skyrocketed. Bars that used to serve real beer had to substitute root beer when liquor-free drinks became the legal alternative to booze. As an added bonus, many of the soda brands were used as underground mixers in illegal drinking parties. Ginger ale was a very fashionable mixer in the 20s, as was 7UP, which was invented during Prohibition. So popular in cocktails was that particular lemon-lime soda that when Prohibition was repealed in 1933, 7UP was heavily marketed as a mixer.

During Prohibition convenience drove the soda industry. Vending machines were created that dispensed sodas into a cup so that workers could get their brand-name refreshment on the job, and six-pack cartons made it easy to carry home several bottles of soda at once. Thirsty consumers were bombarded with a variety of new flavors, and as the country was about to go to war, metal cans were introduced. Metal cans were lighter and more durable than bottles, but at that time the metal was more costly than glass, plus it made the drinks taste funny.

The can problems were fixed after the war, and in 1957 the first lightweight aluminum cans were used to package sodas. It took old customers some time to adjust to the new metal containers, but today more sodas are sold in cans than any other way.

The plastic bottles introduced in the 70s are now the second most common package for sodas, with glass bottles practically fading into obscurity.

These days the cocaine is gone from Coke, Pespi is pepsin-free, and 7UP comes without the attitude-adjusting benefits of lithium. When we drink these drinks today it's usually because we're thirsty. Or we need to get kicked up a notch by the caffeine that's still added to several brands. Whatever the motivation, Joe Average American will knock back over 50 gallons of soda this year, all by himself. With more than 450 different varieties now competing for attention, it's no wonder soft drink ads are every-where we turn.

Choosing which of the most popular sodas to clone for this book was fairly easy: I picked the most successful brand of the most popular flavors (in other words, Coke instead of Pepsi). I would have preferred to create these recipes using the original product's syrup without dilution, since it's really the syrup that we're cloning. But that wasn't always possible. Most of the time, I had to use the original product right out of the bottle or can, as you find it in any store. Then I worked backward, concentrating the flavors, to develop thick, sweet syrup that could be made from scratch.

When the syrup's done, the soda's done. When you've cooled off your syrup and are ready to have a drink, simply add the proper amount of flavored syrup to cold soda water, just as the jerks did (c'mon, that's what they were called) at the soda fountains of yesteryear. Give the drink a little stir, add some ice, and you've just used an old-fashioned technique to re-create one of today's most popular beverages.

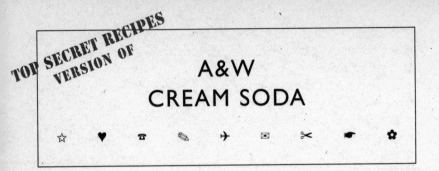

A&W
CREAM SODA

Sure, Roy Allen and Frank Wright are better known for their exquisite root beer concoction sold first from California drive-up stands under the A&W brand name. But these days the company makes a darn good vanilla cream soda as well. And the formula is one that we can easily clone at home just by combining a few simple ingredients. Most of the flavor comes from vanilla, but you'll also need a little lemonade flavor Kool-Aid unsweetened drink mix powder. This mix comes in .23-ounce packets and provides the essential citric acid that gives this soda clone the necessary tang of the real thing. Once you make the syrup, let it cool down in the fridge, then just combine the syrup with cold soda water in a 1 to 4 ratio, add a little ice, and get sipping.

1 ⅓ cups granulated sugar
⅛ teaspoon Kool-Aid lemonade
   unsweetened drink mix
1 cup very hot water
1 cup corn syrup

½ teaspoon plus ¼ teaspoon
   vanilla extract

10 cups cold soda water

1. Dissolve the sugar and Kool-Aid drink mix in the hot water in a small pitcher.
2. Add the corn syrup and vanilla extract and stir well. Cover and chill syrup until cold.
3. When the syrup is cold, pour ¼ cup syrup into 1 cup cold soda water. Stir gently, add ice, and serve.

• MAKES 10 10-OUNCE SERVINGS.

A&W
ROOT BEER

☆ ♥ ☎ ✎ ✈ ✉ ✂ ☞ ✿

In 1919, when Roy Allen and Frank Wright started selling their new root beer beverage to a thirsty America, national Prohibition was taking its grip on the country. Their timing couldn't have been better. No longer able to legally drink real beer, thirsty patriots had to settle for this sweet, foamy concoction derived from roots, herbs, and berries. Roy and Frank had thirteen years of Prohibition to make their mark and their fortune from this refreshing drink. By 1933, when Prohibition came to a screeching halt, Roy and Frank had 171 stands in various shapes and sizes, each with the familiar A&W logo on them, all across the country. These drive-up stands with their tray boys and tray girls bringing cold drinks out to the cars were an inspiration for many other roadside stands and diners, and the prelude to the popular fast food drive-thrus of today. You can still get a foamy mug of A&W root beer at outlets across the country, or just enjoy some from a 12-ounce can.

But if it's some home cloning you'd like to get into, check out this improved version of A&W Root Beer that was first printed in *More Top Secret Recipes*. The beauty is you won't have to worry about collecting roots, herbs, and berries like the pros do. Instead you just need to get some root beer extract, manufactured by McCormick, that you'll find near the vanilla in your local supermarket. Make up some root beer syrup, let it cool off in the fridge, and you can whip up 10 servings by combining the syrup with cold soda water whenever you're ready to drink. Cool, eh?

1 1/3 cups granulated sugar
1 cup very hot water
1 cup corn syrup

1 teaspoon McCormick root beer concentrate

10 cups cold soda water

1. Dissolve the sugar in the hot water in a small pitcher.
2. Add the corn syrup and root beer concentrate and stir well. Cover and chill syrup until cold.
3. When the syrup is cold, pour 1/4 cup syrup into 1 cup of cold soda water. Stir gently, add ice, and serve.

- MAKES 10 10-OUNCE SERVINGS.

COCA-COLA

☆ ♥ ☎ ✎ ✈ ✉ ✂ ☞ ✿

When Atlanta pharmacist John Pemberton whipped up his first cocaine-laced drink he was actually cloning Vin Mariani, a coca leaf–infused red wine that had been selling successfully in Europe since 1863. John's version—called "Pemberton's French wine coca"—had cocaine and wine in it too, but John added kola nut extract to give the drink additional kick (as if it needed it) from the stimulant alkaloid caffeine. Shortly after John had perfected his new drink, local Prohibition hit Atlanta in 1886, and the booze had to come out. The wine was replaced with sugar syrup to make it sweet along with some citric acid for tang, and the name of the new drink was changed to "Coca-Cola," representing the beverage's two very stimulating ingredients. As enthusiasm for cocaine-based tonics waned toward the end of the century, Coca-Cola manufacturers were again forced to ditch another key ingredient. By 1903, the cocaine in Coca-Cola had to come out too.

Although it was a major change to the recipe, removing cocaine from Coca-Cola didn't alter the beverage enough to keep it from becoming the world's number one fountain and bottled soft drink over the years. People enjoyed the drink for its refreshing taste. And, the drink did, after all, still contain enough caffeine to provide a sufficient spring to the step. The drink's success spawned many clones from competitors with only slight variations on the formula's top secret taste, but none, including Pepsi, would become as big a phenomenon as Coke. Many recipes were floating around at the time. It is well documented that John.

sold several copies of the original recipe along with shares in his company to help him through the morphine addiction and poverty that plagued his later years. John died at age 57 in 1888 from stomach cancer before knowing the enormous success of his creation.

Although the drink is 99 percent sugar water, that other 1 percent is the key to the drink's unique taste. The tangy citrus flavors, from lime juice, citrus oils, and citric acid (today the citric acid has been replaced with phosphoric acid), was used by John to overcome the inherent unpleasant bitterness of cocaine and caffeine. Even after removing the coca from the drink, it was still necessary to conceal the ghastly flavor of kola nut caffeine from the taste buds with the sweet, tangy syrup.

To make an accurate clone of Coca-Cola at home I started with the medicinal ingredient, probably just as John did. But rather than harvesting kola nuts, we have the luxury of access to caffeine pills found in any grocery store or pharmacy. One such brand is Vivarin, but it is yellow in color with a thick coating and it tastes much too bitter. NoDoz, however, is white and less bitter, with a thinner coating. Each NoDoz tablet contains 200 milligrams of caffeine, and a 12-ounce serving of Coke has 46 milligrams in it. So if we use 8 NoDoz tablets that have been crushed to powder with a mortar and pestle (or in a bowl using the back of a spoon) we get 44 milligrams of caffeine in a 12-ounce serving, or 36 milligrams in each of the 10-ounce servings we make with this recipe.

Finding and adding the caffeine is the easy part. You'll probably have more trouble obtaining Coke's crucial flavoring ingredient: cassia oil. I was hoping to leave such a hard-to-get ingredient out of this recipe, but I found it impossible. The unique flavor of Coke absolutely requires the inclusion of this Vietnamese cinnamon oil (usually sold for aromatherapy), but only a very small amount. You'll find the cassia oil in a health food store (I used the brand Oshadhi), along with the lemon oil and orange oil. The yield of this recipe had to be cranked up to 44 10-ounce servings since these oils are so strong—just one drop of each is all you'll need. Find them in bottles that allow you to measure exactly one drop if you can. If the oils don't come in such a bottle, buy eyedroppers at a drug store. Before you leave the health food store, don't forget the citric acid.

This recipe, because of the old-fashioned technique of adding the syrup to soda water, creates a clone of Coke as it would taste coming out of a fountain machine. That Coke is usually not as fizzy as the bottled stuff. But if you add some ice to a glass of bottled Coke, and then some to this cloned version, the bubbles will settle down and you'll discover how close the two are.

Because subtle difference in flavor can affect the finished product, be sure to measure your ingredients very carefully. Use the flat top edge of a butter knife to scrape away the excess sugar and citric acid from the top of the measuring cup and teaspoon, and don't estimate on any of the liquid ingredients.

6 cups granulated sugar
2 cups (one 16-ounce bottle) light corn syrup
8 NoDoz tablets, crushed to powder
2 teaspoons citric acid
7 cups boiling water
1 tablespoon lime juice
½ teaspoon vanilla
1 drop lemon oil

1 drop orange oil
1 drop cinnamon (cassia) oil

COLOR
1 tablespoon red food coloring
1½ teaspoons yellow food coloring
½ teaspoon blue food coloring
18 drops green food coloring

44 cups cold soda water

1. Combine sugar, corn syrup, powdered NoDoz, and citric acid in a large pitcher or bowl. Add the boiling water, and stir until the sugar has dissolved and the solution is clear. Strain the syrup through a paper towel–lined strainer to remove the NoDoz sediment.
2. Add the lime juice, vanilla, lemon oil, orange oil, and cassia oil to the syrup and stir.
3. Add the colors to the syrup, then cover it and chill it for several hours until cold.
4. To make the soda, add ¼ cup of cold syrup to 1 cup of cold soda water. Stir gently, drop in some ice, and serve.

• MAKES 44 10-OUNCE SERVINGS.

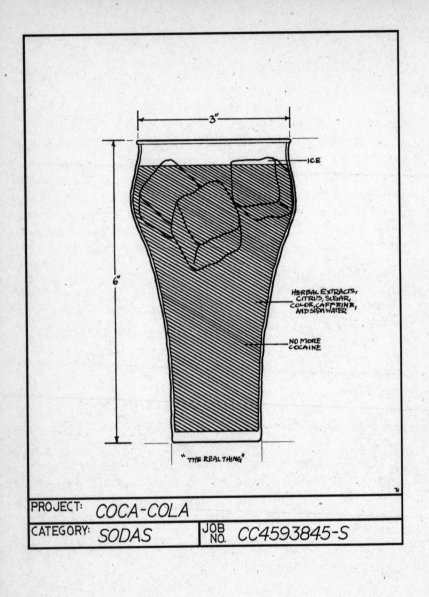

3"

ICE

6"

HERBAL EXTRACTS,
CITRUS, SUGAR,
COLOR, CAFFEINE,
AND SODA WATER

NO MORE
COCAINE

" THE REAL THING"

PROJECT:	COCA-COLA		
CATEGORY: SODAS		JOB NO.	CC4593845-S

ORANGE SLICE

☆ ♥ ☎ ✎ ✈ ✉ ✂ ☞ ✿

To make your own version of the syrup for this orange soda that comes to us from the Pepsi-Cola Company, you need to combine a simple syrup recipe with two popular versions of dry orange drink mix: Kool-Aid orange unsweetened drink mix and Tang. But unlike the real thing that "contains no juice," your homemade version includes a bit of real orange juice solids that come powdered into every scoop of Tang mix. After you make the syrup, be sure to let it cool in the refrigerator before you combine it with cold soda water to make a perfect finished product.

1 cup granulated sugar
1 cup corn syrup
1 0.15-ounce package Kool-Aid orange unsweetened drink mix

1 tablespoon Tang orange drink mix
1¼ cups boiling water

8 cups cold soda water

1. Combine sugar, corn syrup, and drink mix powders in a medium pitcher or bowl. Add boiling water and stir until sugar has dissolved and syrup is clear. Cover and chill this syrup for several hours until cold.
2. To make the soda, add ⅓ cup of cold syrup to 1 cup of cold soda water (1 to 3 ratio). Stir gently, drop in some ice, and serve.

• MAKES 8 13-OUNCE SERVINGS.

7UP

☆ ♥ ☎ ✎ ✈ ⌧ ✂ ☛ ✿

It was the perfect drink for a Great Depression. In 1929, the United States slipped into a giant economic slump, and a new lemon-lime soda with an attitude-adjusting additive was rolled out. The drink's slogan, "Takes the Ouch Out of the Grouch," referred to lithium, a powerful drug used to treat manic depression and prevent mood swings. Lithium was added to every serving of 7UP until the mid-1940s.

The soda wasn't called 7UP at first. The drink, created by Charles Leiper Grigg, was originally called Bib-Labeled Lithiated Lemon-Lime Soda, but that name, and even the abbreviated version, BLLLLS, was too long.

Today, no one can agree on the origin of the name 7UP. Some theorize that it came from the number of ingredients in the soda, while others say it came from the size of the 7-ounce bottles in which the drink was first sold. There are even theories that the name came from a popular card game at the time called 7UP, or from a cattle brand Charlie Grigg saw one day.

During the sugar rationing of World War II, 7UP was especially popular with bottlers since it used less sugar than other soft drinks. In 1967, the company introduced the famous "uncola" ads, with an image of the drink served in an upside-down bell-shaped cola glass. That campaign continued through the 70s with deep-throated actor Geoffrey Holder explaining the secret of the drink to be the "uncola nut."

The slogan "follow the liter" was later developed to announce 7UP's new packaging in 1-liter bottles. Soon afterward, every major soft drink label was selling their sodas in metric bottles.

In 1986, the Seven Up Company merged with the Dr Pepper Company, creating the world's third-largest soft drink company behind Coca-Cola and Pepsi.

Now you can make a home clone for this refreshing citrus beverage in no time at all. Just add lemon and lime juice to a syrup solution, along with a little Kool-Aid lemonade drink mix for that special tang (thanks to included citric acid), and you're almost there. When the syrup has cooled, you just mix it into some cold soda water in a 1 to 4 ratio. And that's it. You've just made this clone of 7UP yours.

1 cup plus 1 tablespoon granulated sugar	1 ¼ cups very hot water
1 cup corn syrup	1 tablespoon bottled lime juice
½ teaspoon Kool-Aid lemonade unsweetened drink mix	2 teaspoons bottled lemon juice
	11 cups cold soda water

1. Combine sugar, corn syrup, and lemonade drink mix in a medium pitcher or bowl. Add hot water and stir until sugar has dissolved and syrup is clear.
2. Add lime juice and lemon juice and stir. Cover and chill for several hours until cold.
3. To make the soda, add ¼ cup of cold syrup to 1 cup of cold soda water (1 to 4 ratio). Stir gently, drop in some ice, and serve.

• MAKES 11 10-OUNCE SERVINGS.

SONIC DRIVE-IN CHERRY LIMEADE

☆　♥　☎　✎　✈　✉　✂　☛　❀

Here's the signature drink from the chain that's reviving the drive-in burger joint, just like a scene out of *American Graffiti* or *Happy Days*.

It was in 1953 that Troy Smith obtained the parcel of land in Shawnee, Oklahoma, that was big enough to fit the new steakhouse and root beer stand that was his dream. Troy thought he'd make the steakhouse his primary operation, but as it turned out folks preferred the hot dogs and cold drinks over at the root beer stand. So Troy did the smart thing and ditched the steakhouse to focus all his efforts on the other joint. At first he called the root beer stand "Top Hat," but when Troy found out later that name was already being used, he came up with "Sonic" to signify "service at the speed of sound." Today the chain is the sixth-largest hamburger outlet in the country.

This recipe makes a simple, old-fashioned drink by combining Sprite with cherry juice and some lime wedges. Use cherry juice made by Libby under the brand name Juicy Juice for the best clone.

12 ounces cold Sprite (1 can)　　¼ cup cherry juice (Libby's Juicy
3 lime wedges (⅛ of a lime each)　　Juice is best)

1. Fill a 16-ounce glass ⅔ full with ice.
2. Pour Sprite over the ice.
3. Add the juice of three lime wedges and drop them into the drink.
4. Add the cherry juice and serve with a straw.

• MAKES 1 16-OUNCE DRINK (MEDIUM SIZE).

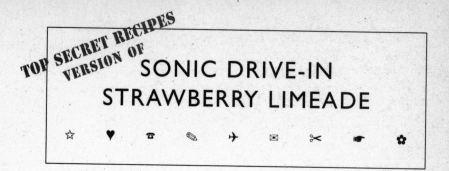

SONIC DRIVE-IN
STRAWBERRY LIMEADE

Troy Smith isn't the one who came up with the idea to use an intercom system in the parking lot so that customers could pull up to order, and then eat while still in their cars. He was inspired by another hamburger stand he saw while driving through Louisiana, and had the same system designed for his place. Troy's borrowed concept survived the generations thanks to a menu of food with wide appeal. Today Sonic is the only major fast food chain still incorporating the nearly 50-year-old service concept. And just as in the 50s, roller-skating carhops still bring the food right to the car window so diners can stay comfortably seated behind the wheel.

This is a flavor variation of Sonic's signature Cherry Limeade. This version is just as good, even with the minor inconvenience of little chunks of strawberry clogging up the straw.

12 ounces cold Sprite (1 can)
3 lime wedges (⅛ of a lime each)

2 tablespoons frozen sweetened
    sliced strawberries, thawed

1. Fill a 16-ounce glass ⅔ full with ice.
2. Pour Sprite over the ice.
3. Add the juice of three lime wedges.
4. Add two tablespoons of strawberries with the syrup. Serve with a straw.

• MAKES 1 16-OUNCE DRINK (MEDIUM SIZE).

SONIC DRIVE-IN
OCEAN WATER

Any Sonic Drive-In regular knows the four or five unique fountain drink favorites on the menu. There's the Limeade, the Diet Limeade, Strawberry Limeade, and, of course, the Cherry Limeade. But that bright blue stuff called Ocean Water has become a recent favorite for anyone who digs the taste of coconut— it's like a pina colada soda. The server simply squirts a bit of blue coconut-flavored syrup into a cup of cold Sprite. The big secret to duplicating this one at home is re-creating that syrup, so that's the first step. After that's done, you make the drink as they do at the restaurant in less time than it takes to say, "Does my blue tongue clash with what I'm wearing?"

3 tablespoons water
2 tablespoons sugar
1 teaspoon imitation coconut
   extract

2 drops blue food coloring
2 12-ounce cans cold Sprite
ice

1. Combine the water and the sugar in a small bowl. Microwave for 30 to 45 seconds, and then stir to dissolve all of the sugar. Allow this syrup to cool.
2. Add coconut extract and food coloring to the cooled syrup. Stir well.
3. Combine the syrup with two 12-ounce cans of cold Sprite. Divide and pour over ice. Add straws and serve.

- MAKES 2 12-OUNCE SERVINGS.

SQUIRT

☆　♥　☎　✎　✈　✉　✂　☞　✿

Soda and citrus flavors were combined in 1938 to create a grapefruit-lemon soft drink that would later inspire Coke to make Fresca. Fresca was popular when it was introduced in the 60s since it was artificially sweetened and contained no calories. That was back when diet drinks were just catching on. Nowadays just about every soda comes in a diet version, and Fresca sales have slipped, despite a tweaking of the formula in the early 90s.

Squirt continues to hold on to a loyal cult following, with many who claim the soda is the only true cure for a hangover. To clone it, just add real bottled white grapefruit juice, along with a little Kool-Aid mix for a lemony tang, to the simple syrup recipe. Chill the syrup and soda water until cold and get ready to make a dozen cups' worth of citrus soda at home.

1½ cups granulated sugar
⅛ teaspoon Kool-Aid lemonade
   unsweetened drink mix
¼ cup boiling water

1 cup corn syrup
1½ cups white grapefruit juice

12 cups cold soda water

1. Combine sugar and Kool-Aid mix with the boiling water in a medium pitcher or bowl. Stir well. Add corn syrup and stir.
2. Add grapefruit juice and stir until sugar crystals are dissolved. Cover and chill for several hours until cold.
3. To make the soda, stir the syrup first, then add ¼ cup of cold syrup to 1 cup of cold soda water (1 to 4 ratio). Stir gently, drop in some ice, and serve.

- MAKES 12 10-OUNCE SERVINGS.

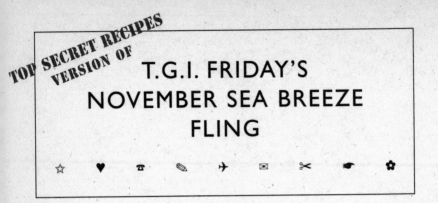

T.G.I. FRIDAY'S NOVEMBER SEA BREEZE FLING

Not only does the restaurant still serve some of the tastiest cocktails and mixed drinks, but Friday's also has one of the best darn selections of custom non-alcoholic drinks in the business. The smoothies and shakes at Friday's are all excellent, as are the designer sodas called "Flings." These are hand-mixed soda beverages made in a fashion reminiscent of old-time soda fountains. Juices and sweeteners are mixed with cold soda water and served elegantly over ice—you can't go wrong with one of these. The Fling cloned here uses cranberry juice, apple juice, simple syrup, and sweet & sour mix. If you've got the time, make the sweet & sour from scratch using the recipe at the back of the book.

1 ½ ounces cranberry juice
1 ½ ounces apple juice
1 ½ ounces sweet & sour mix
   (bottled or use the recipe from page 231)

½ ounce simple syrup (from page 226)
1 ½ ounces club soda

GARNISH
lime wedge

1. Fill a 14-ounce glass with ice.
2. Pour juices, sweet & sour mix, and simple syrup into a shaker and shake well.
3. Pour drink over the ice, add a lime wedge and the club soda on top, and serve with a straw.

• MAKES 1 DRINK.

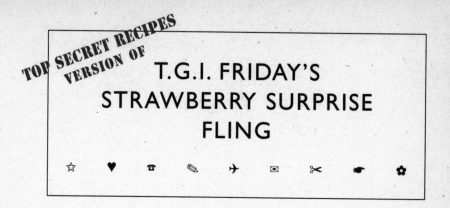

T.G.I. FRIDAY'S STRAWBERRY SURPRISE FLING

This version of a Friday's Fling is more tropical than the preceding recipe and doesn't require simple syrup. When you're ready to be flung, get some of the sweetened sliced strawberries out of the freezer and start thawing.

2 tablespoons frozen sweetened
   sliced strawberries, thawed
1½ ounces pineapple juice
1½ ounces papaya juice
1½ ounces apple juice

1½ ounces club soda

GARNISH
1 fresh strawberry

1. Fill a 14-ounce glass with ice.
2. Pour strawberries, with syrup, and juices into a shaker and shake well.
3. Pour drink over the ice, and add a fresh strawberry to the rim of the glass. Splash the club soda over the top and serve with a straw.

• MAKES 1 DRINK.

SMOOTHIES

Frozen blended fruit drinks weren't called "smoothies" back in the 20s when Orange Julius first made them popular. That name, and the many different ingredients used in the drinks today, didn't catch on until the 1990s.

The trend toward smoothies as we know them these days may have started in health club shake bars where a wide variety of juices and fruits were mixed with ice, protein powders, and vitamins in a blender. Sometimes ice cream, frozen yogurt, or sorbet was added to the mix to give the drink a smooth texture.

These juice bars would eventually break away from the health clubs and become independently run outlets or large chains, such as Jamba Juice. Soon, established ice cream chains such as Baskin-Robbins and Dairy Queen were offering their own versions of smoothies, and today the drink is everywhere.

You can make smoothies very easily at home with the same type of ingredients the pros use, as long as you have a blender. Professional smoothie makers have blenders designed specifically for the job. Industrial-strength models speed up and slow down automatically and stop on cue when the drink is just right. These machines make the job much easier for the cats behind the counter when multiple orders are flying in.

You can use a regular home blender, though, to create perfect smoothies like those you get at a chain. You may have to stop your machine once in a while to stir things up a bit with a long-handled spoon, but when the ice is all crushed and the drink is smooth, you will have re-created the refreshing smoothie experience without waiting in any pesky lines.

APPLEBEE'S BANANABERRY FREEZE

Ah, if only kitchen cloning were an exact science. While researching this one I saw the same bartender make the drink two different ways on two different days. Only after a firm grilling did I get her to admit to her personal "improvement" to the chain's secret recipe. The official clone includes the ingredients found below. But if you want to add a little pineapple juice—as some independent-thinking bartenders are apt to do—you might discover you have indeed created a tastier version of this refreshing smoothie. On that day the cloning gods shall be looking the other way.

But, for heaven's sake, be sure your banana is soft and ripe. This is a detail the gods won't ignore.

1 10-ounce box frozen sweetened
   sliced strawberries, thawed
⅓ cup pina colada mix (from
   recipe on page 230)
2 cups ice
2 ripe bananas

GARNISH
whipped cream
2 fresh strawberries

1. Use a blender to puree the entire contents of the thawed box of frozen strawberries.
2. Add ⅓ cup pina colada mix and 2 cups of ice to the blender.
3. Cut the end off each banana—set these pieces aside to use later as a garnish—then put the bananas into the blender.
4. Blend on high speed until the ice is crushed and the drink is

smooth. Pour into two tall stemmed glasses, such as daiquiri glasses.

5. Slice each strawberry halfway up through the middle and add one to the rim of each glass.

6. Cut each banana slice halfway through the middle and add one to the rim of each glass next to the strawberry. Top with whipped cream and serve with a straw.

• MAKES 2 DRINKS.

BASKINS-ROBBINS PEACH SMOOTHIE

☆　♥　☎　✎　✈　✉　✄　☞　✿

Dairy Queen's got twice as many stores, but Baskin-Robbins is still the country's second-largest ice cream chain with around 2,500 outlets spread across the nation. And, naturally, when the chain known for its 31 flavors of ice cream noticed the smoothie craze building in 1997, it hopped right on board with its own selection made from sherbet or vanilla fat-free frozen yogurt. In the stores, servers use a pineapple juice concentrate for this smoothie, but we can still get a great clone by using the more popular canned pineapple juice found in any supermarket. As for the peaches, you may want to let them thaw a bit and then chop them up so you can get a more accurate measure.

1 cup pineapple juice
¾ cup frozen peaches, sliced

1 scoop fat-free vanilla frozen
　yogurt
3 or 4 ice cubes

Combine all ingredients in a blender and blend on high speed until all the ice is crushed and the drink is smooth.

• MAKES 1 16-OUNCE DRINK.

BASKIN-ROBBINS
STRAWBERRY SMOOTHIE

☆　♥　☎　✎　✈　✉　✂　☛　✿

When Irv Robbins was discharged from the army in 1945, he hooked up with his brother-in-law Burt Baskin and the two opened an ice cream parlor in Glendale, California. A simple coin flip determined whose name would go first on the sign. By 1948 six Baskin-Robbins stores had opened their doors and the concept of franchising in the ice cream industry was born.

As in the previous recipe, you may want to let the fruit thaw out a bit here so that you can chop up the strawberries and get a more accurate measure. The word on the street is that some of those frozen whole strawberries can be quite big. Chopping them up first also helps you get a smoother blend going.

1 cup Kern's strawberry nectar
¾ cup frozen whole strawberries, chopped

1 scoop fat-free vanilla frozen yogurt
3 or 4 ice cubes

Combine all ingredients in a blender and blend on high speed until all the ice is crushed and the drink is smooth.

• MAKES 1 16-OUNCE DRINK.

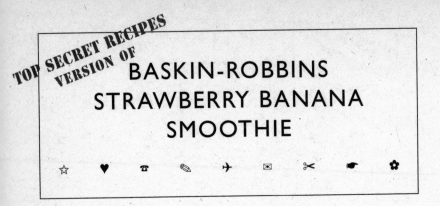

BASKIN-ROBBINS STRAWBERRY BANANA SMOOTHIE

It was in 1953 that the now-famous "31 Flavors" sign was introduced, burdening customers with the dilemma of having to decide which of so many great ice cream flavors they would choose. The number 31 was picked to suggest that a new flavor could be selected every day of the month. The company has come up with around one thousand flavors so far. And as with their most famous flavor, Rocky Road, many other Baskin-Robbins flavor creations would be often imitated—among them Pralines and Cream and Jamoca Almond Fudge.

This recipe for a smoothie is very similar to the previous clone, the only difference being a reduction in strawberries and the addition of half of a ripe banana. You may want to chop up those frozen strawberries (especially the big 'uns) to make measuring easier and more accurate.

1 cup Kern's strawberry nectar
½ cup frozen whole strawberries,
  chopped
1 scoop fat-free vanilla frozen
  yogurt

½ ripe banana
3 or 4 ice cubes

Combine all ingredients in a blender and blend on high speed until all the ice is crushed and the drink is smooth.

• MAKES 1 16-OUNCE DRINK.

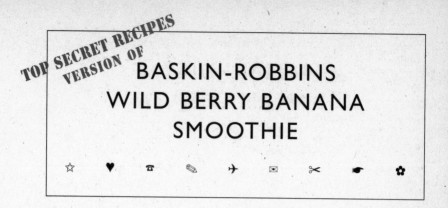

BASKIN-ROBBINS
WILD BERRY BANANA
SMOOTHIE

Baskin-Robbins has become known for creating flavors representing the events of the day. When the Brooklyn Dodgers
moved to Los Angeles, the chain introduced "Baseball Nut."
When James Bond films were popular in the 60s, the chain rolled
out "0031 Secret Bonded Flavor." When the TV show *Laugh-In* became a big hit, the company created "Here Comes the Fudge."
And when Americans landed on the moon, Baskin-Robbins cele-
brated with "Lunar Cheesecake."

This smoothie clone is the only one of the four represented
here to use some raspberry sherbet along with the vanilla frozen
yogurt. It's the most complex of Baskin-Robbins' smoothie selections, but worth every bit of extra effort.

1 cup pineapple juice
½ cup frozen blueberries
½ scoop fat-free vanilla frozen
   yogurt

½ scoop raspberry sherbet
½ ripe banana
3 or 4 ice cubes

Combine all ingredients in a blender and blend on high speed until all the ice is crushed and the drink is smooth.

• MAKES 1 16-OUNCE DRINK.

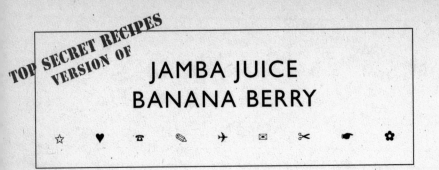

JAMBA JUICE
BANANA BERRY

Jamba Juice has become America's favorite smoothie chain, with tasty fruit-filled blends served up in giant 24-ounce cups at over 325 stores. Appreciate the ease with which you are able to suck down your next Jamba Juice smoothie, since the wide straws at the chain have been through rigorous "suckability factor" testing to ensure that the good stuff gets all the way through to your gullet.

¾ cup apple juice
¾ cup Kern's strawberry nectar
⅔ cup frozen blueberries
1 sliced banana

1 scoop raspberry sherbet
1 scoop fat-free vanilla frozen
   yogurt
1 cup ice

Combine all ingredients in a blender and blend on high speed until all the ice is crushed and the drink is smooth.

• Makes 1 24-ounce drink.

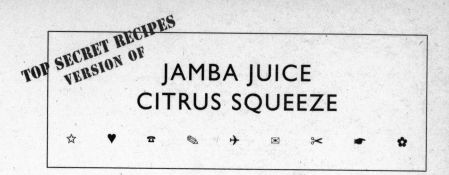

JAMBA JUICE
CITRUS SQUEEZE

This smoothie is a very popular choice among the more than 16 varieties of smoothies made fresh at this smoothie chain. If your blender stalls out on you from the thickness of the drink, stop it and stir with a long spoon. That should get things going again. For the perfect clone, you want to be sure all the ice is crushed so that the drink is smooth-a-licious.

1 cup fresh orange juice
½ cup pineapple juice
⅔ cup frozen whole strawberries
1 sliced banana

2 scoops orange sherbet
1 cup ice

Combine all ingredients in a blender and blend on high speed until all the ice is crushed and the drink is smooth.

• Makes 1 24-ounce drink.

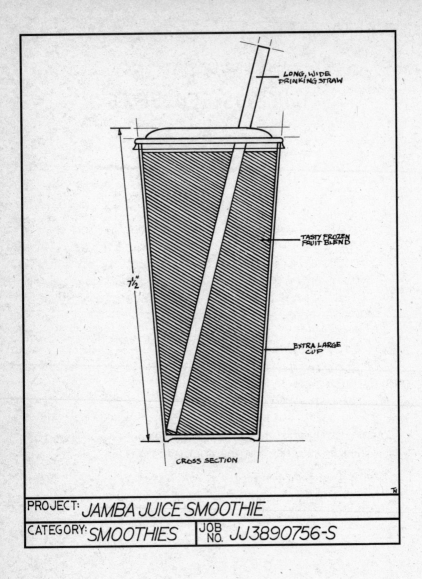

LONG, WIDE
DRINKING STRAW

TASTY FROZEN
FRUIT BLEND

EXTRA LARGE
CUP

$7\frac{1}{2}$"

CROSS SECTION

TW

PROJECT: *JAMBA JUICE SMOOTHIE*

CATEGORY: *SMOOTHIES* JOB NO. *JJ3890756-S*

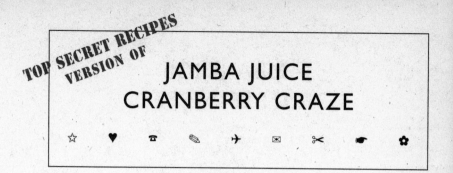

JAMBA JUICE
CRANBERRY CRAZE

☆　♥　☎　✎　✈　✉　✂　☞　✿

The menu description says that this drink includes plain nonfat yogurt (not the frozen kind), but I noticed that the server at the store I visited didn't put it in. When I asked her if she forgot the ingredient, she told me they don't include the yogurt anymore, even if the board says otherwise. Okay, right. So, while the menu might insist that this smoothie includes plain yogurt, today we make our clone without it.

1 ½ cups cranberry juice
½ cup frozen whole strawberries
¼ cup frozen blueberries

2 scoops raspberry sherbet
1 cup ice

Combine all ingredients in a blender and blend on high speed until all the ice is crushed and the drink is smooth.

- MAKES 1 24-OUNCE DRINK.

JAMBA JUICE
ORANGE-A-PEEL

☆ ♥ ☎ ✏ ✈ ✉ ✂ ☞ ✿

Pick your juice wisely. For this smoothie Jamba Juice squeezes whole oranges with a handy orange squeezing machine in each store. So if it's the addicting taste of the real thing you're shooting for, be sure to get your orange juice freshly squeezed or squish some out yourself.

1 ½ cups fresh orange juice
⅔ cup frozen whole strawberries
1 sliced banana

2 scoops fat-free vanilla frozen
   yogurt
1 cup ice

Combine all ingredients in a blender and blend on high speed until all the ice is crushed and the drink is smooth.

• MAKES 1 24-OUNCE DRINK.

JAMBA JUICE
PEACH PLEASURE

☆   ♥   ☎   ✎   ✈   ✉   ✂   ☞   ✿

Jamba Juice got its start as "Juice Club" in San Luis Obispo, California. Early success with healthy food and juice blends led to quick growth with more stores and eventually a name change in 1995. The company claims "Jamba" means "to celebrate," just as your tastebuds do when they get a load of a smoothie like the one this recipe clones. It uses an entire can of Kern's peach nectar plus frozen peaches, banana, and some orange sherbet. Tastebuds, party on.

12 ounces Kern's peach nectar   ½ ripe banana
   (1 can)   2 scoops orange sherbet
1 cup frozen peaches   1 cup ice

Combine all ingredients in a blender and blend on high speed until all the ice is crushed and the drink is smooth.

• MAKES 1 24-OUNCE DRINK.

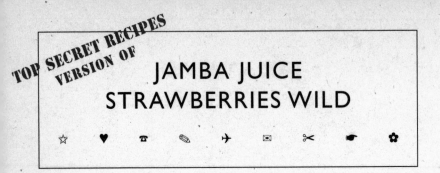

JAMBA JUICE
STRAWBERRIES WILD

☆   ♥   ☎   ✎   ✈   ✉   ✂   ☞   ✿

One of the most popular smoothie combinations around is strawberry-banana. This clone imitates Jamba's version, which adds apple juice and vanilla frozen yogurt to the mix. Look for the strawberry nectar in the juice aisle and warm up the blender.

¾ cup apple juice
¾ cup Kern's strawberry nectar
⅔ cup frozen whole strawberries
1 sliced banana

2 scoops fat-free vanilla frozen
  yogurt
1 cup ice

Combine all ingredients in a blender and blend on high speed until all the ice is crushed and the drink is smooth.

• MAKES 1 24-OUNCE DRINK.

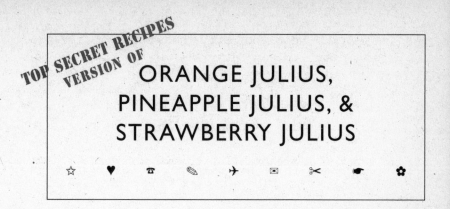

ORANGE JULIUS, PINEAPPLE JULIUS, & STRAWBERRY JULIUS

☆　♥　☎　✎　✈　⊠　✂　☛　✿

Coffeehouses have replaced many of the old Orange Julius stands, but there's still a nostalgic group of us who long for the frothy juice drinks invented decades ago by Julius Freed. Today Orange Julius has tailored its business to meet the changing demands of customers by including several varieties of fruit drinks and updated smoothies on its menu. But it's the foamy fruit juice creation developed in the late twenties that made the company famous, and that's what I've cloned here in improved versions of the recipes found in *Top Secret Recipes* and *More Top Secret Recipes*. The flavor and consistency are better now, plus we use the blender to dissolve the sugar before adding the ice. Use pasteurized egg whites found packaged in your local supermarket or just use egg substitute, which is also made from pasteurized egg whites.

ORANGE JULIUS

1 ¼ cups orange juice
1 cup water
3 tablespoons egg white or egg
　substitute

1 teaspoon vanilla extract
¼ cup granulated sugar
1 ½ cups ice

Combine all of the ingredients except ice in a blender and blend on high speed for 15 to 20 seconds or until the sugar is dissolved.

Add the ice and blend for another 10 to 15 seconds or so, until ice is mostly crushed yet still a bit coarse.

• MAKES 2 16-OUNCE DRINKS.

PINEAPPLE JULIUS

1 8-ounce can crushed pineapple
   in juice
1 cup water
3 tablespoons egg white or egg
   substitute

1 teaspoon vanilla extract
¼ cup granulated sugar
1½ cups ice

Combine all of the ingredients except ice in a blender and blend on high speed for 15 to 20 seconds or until the sugar is dissolved. Add the ice and blend for another 10 to 15 seconds or so, until ice is mostly crushed yet still a bit coarse.

• MAKES 2 16-OUNCE DRINKS.

STRAWBERRY JULIUS

1 cup frozen sliced strawberries,
   thawed (1 10-ounce box)
1 cup water
3 tablespoons egg white or egg
   substitute

1 teaspoon vanilla extract
¼ cup granulated sugar
1½ cups ice

Combine all of the ingredients except ice in a blender and blend on high speed for 15 to 20 seconds or until the sugar is dissolved. Add the ice and blend for another 10 to 15 seconds or so, until ice is mostly crushed yet still a bit coarse.

• MAKES 2 16-OUNCE DRINKS.

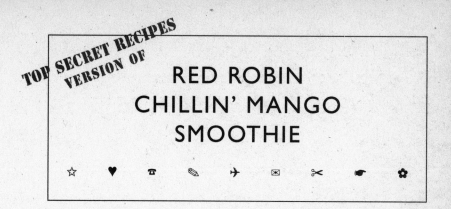

RED ROBIN CHILLIN' MANGO SMOOTHIE

Masterful mixologists make this drink as a special limited-time-only summer refresher at the popular eatery. The chain uses a special pureed mango fruit mix made by Torani, the same company that makes the flavoring syrups used in coffeehouses. But since this special ingredient can be hard to come by, we'll substitute with canned mango chunks that you'll find in jars in the produce section.

¾ cup canned mango, with juice
¾ ounce grenadine
¼ cup orange juice
1 cup ice

GARNISH
orange wedge
maraschino cherry

1. Combine all ingredients in a blender on high speed and mix until smooth.
2. Pour into a 12-ounce glass, then add an orange wedge and maraschino cherry speared on a toothpick. Serve with a straw.

• MAKES 1 DRINK.

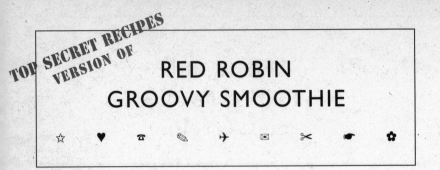

RED ROBIN
GROOVY SMOOTHIE

The strawberries used for this drink come in 10-ounce boxes in the freezer section of your local supermarket. These berries work great because when thawed they wind up swimming in a juicy sweet syrup that's perfect for this clone recipe. The restaurant adds a special blend of apple, raspberry, and blackberry juices called "Groovy Mix" to the drink, but we can still create an excellent carbon copy using a blend of apple and berry juices made by Langer's. If you can't find that brand, use any berry juice blend you can get your hands on and you'll still have an extremely groovy drink.

⅓ cup frozen sweetened sliced
   strawberries, thawed
½ ripe banana
⅓ cup Langer's berry juice (a
   blend of berry and apple
   juices)
¼ cup Kern's peach nectar

½ cup ice
½ cup vanilla ice cream

GARNISH
orange wedge
maraschino cherry

1. Combine all ingredients in a blender and blend on high speed until smooth. Pour into a 16-ounce glass.
2. Add an orange wedge and a maraschino cherry speared on a toothpick. Serve with a straw.

• MAKES 1 DRINK.

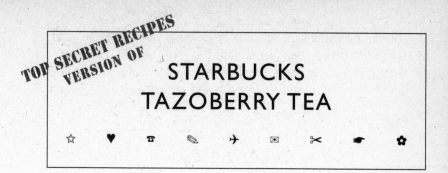

STARBUCKS TAZOBERRY TEA

☆　♥　☎　✎　✈　⊠　✄　☛　✿

Check out the menu board at any Starbucks and you'll find this frozen drink described as a blend of raspberry and other fruit juices plus Starbucks' own Tazo brand tea. We've discovered that those other fruit juices include white grape juice, aroniaberry, cranberry, and blackberry. Since aroniaberry juice is next to impossible to track down in a local supermarket, we'll have to make a taste-alike drink with a combination of just the other, more important flavors. Grab the raspberry syrup and a jar of seedless blackberry jam made by Knott's Berry Farm, and brew up a little tea. Starbucks uses Tazo black tea for the drink, but you can use the more common Lipton tea bags. You will only use ⅓ cup of the tea for this 1-serving recipe, so you'll have plenty left over for additional servings, or for a quick iced tea fix.

4 cups water
1 tea bag
¼ cup Ocean Spray cranberry/
　raspberry juice
2 tablespoons concentrated white
　grape juice, thawed

2 tablespoons Knott's Berry Farm
　raspberry syrup
1 tablespoon Knott's Berry Farm
　seedless blackberry jam
1 teaspoon lemon juice
2 cups ice

1. First brew the tea by bringing 4 cups of water to a rapid boil. Turn off the heat, drop in the tea bag, and let the tea steep for an hour or so. Remove the tea bag and put the tea into the refrigerator to chill.

2. When the tea is cold, make your drink by pouring juices, raspberry syrup, blackberry jam, and ⅓ cup of tea into a blender.
3. Add 2 cups of ice and blend on high speed for 20 to 30 seconds or until the drink is smooth and all ice has been crushed.

• MAKES 1 16-OUNCE SERVING.

TAZOBERRY & CREAM

Some folks like their Tazoberry a little creamier. It's an easy variation that includes adding just 2 tablespoons of cream to the blender with the other ingredients in the recipe above. Blend as described in Step 3, and top the drink off with whipped cream if you've got it.

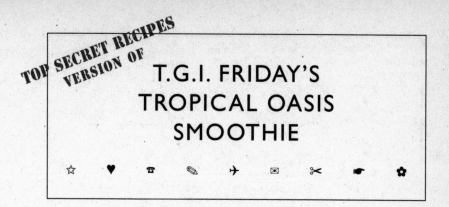

T.G.I. FRIDAY'S TROPICAL OASIS SMOOTHIE

I remember when the menu at T.G.I. Friday's used to include over half a dozen smoothies, but in many Friday's restaurants today the list has been trimmed to just the top few sellers. This is a clone for one of those three favorites. The other two—Gold Medalist and Tropical Runner—are cloned in *Top Secret Restaurant Recipes*.

1/4 cup pineapple juice
1/4 cup papaya juice
1/2 cup canned peaches
1 scoop orange sherbet
1/2 cup ice

GARNISH
orange slice
maraschino cherry

1. Combine all ingredients in a blender and mix on high speed until smooth.
2. Pour into a 14-ounce glass, add an orange slice and maraschino cherry on a toothpick. Serve with a straw.

• MAKES 1 DRINK.

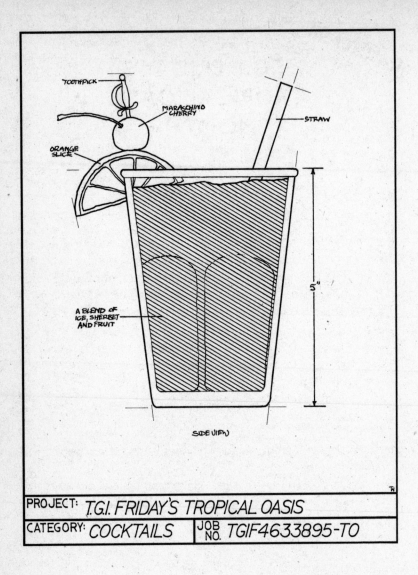

TOOTHPICK

MARASCHINO
CHERRY

STRAW

ORANGE
SLICE

5"

A BLEND OF
ICE, SHERBET
AND FRUIT

SIDE VIEW

PROJECT: *T.G.I. FRIDAY'S TROPICAL OASIS*

CATEGORY: *COCKTAILS*   JOB NO. *TGIF4633895-TO*

SHAKES

To make a milk shake you must use ice cream. I don't care what they say in Rhode Island and parts of Massachusetts where a milk shake is just milk shaken up with flavored syrup. To those folks, when you add ice cream it's called a *cabinet*. And I don't care what they say in other parts of New England where milk shakes are called *velvets* or *frappes*. A milk shake, according to the ultimate food reference guide, *Food Lover's Companion*, "consists of a blended combination of milk, ice cream, and flavored syrup, fruit or other flavorings."

Milk shakes became very popular in the 40s and 50s when machines were developed to dispense a perfectly frozen creamy product. Busy soda fountains and drive-in restaurants welcomed the extra convenience and consistency offered by these handy machines. Ray Kroc, the man who made McDonald's a household name, was once the exclusive distributor of a milk shake machine called the Multimixer. While on his route he heard about a thriving hamburger stand in San Bernardino, California, that was using a row of eight Multimixers at a time to serve lines of people. His initial pitch to the McDonald brothers for franchise rights was motivated by his dream of selling each new store a bunch of these milk shake machines.

In the last decade or so the most popular milk shakes are more than just thin, lightly colored desserts served with a straw. With the success of Dairy Queen's Blizzard, milk shakes have become much thicker and chunkier. Bits of fruit, candy, cookies, and cereal are added to the mix, making for a treat that can no longer be sucked through a straw without collapsing a lung.

The beauty of all these excellent desserts-in-a-cup is that they can be re-created at home without having to go out and get a Multimixer. For most of them, just get out the blender. For the thicker, chunkier shakes (such as the Blizzard and McFlurry clones), you won't even need a blender. Instead you'll use a custom technique developed for this book that incorporates a frozen glass or ceramic bowl. When the ice cream is mixed with milk and other ingredients in the frozen bowl, the ice cream won't melt, creating a thick and creamy finished product that will hold up a spoon.

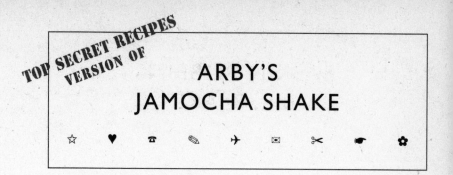

ARBY'S
JAMOCHA SHAKE

Okay, wash out the blender; this one's been begging to be cloned for years now. Arby's famous Jamocha Shake was one of the first frozen coffee drinks to gain popularity, even before Starbucks pummeled us with Frappuccinos. This thick drink is actually more milk shake than coffee drink, but if you like the original, you'll love this easy-to-make clone that serves two.

1 cup cold coffee
1 cup low-fat milk
3 tablespoons granulated sugar

3 cups vanilla ice cream
3 tablespoons chocolate syrup

1. Combine the coffee, milk, and sugar in a blender and mix on medium speed for 15 seconds to dissolve the sugar.
2. Add the ice cream and chocolate syrup, then blend on high speed until smooth and creamy. Stop blender and stir mixture with a spoon if necessary to help blend ingredients.
3. Pour drink into two 16-ounce glasses and serve.

• MAKES 2 LARGE DRINKS.

BASKIN-ROBBINS
B.R. BLAST

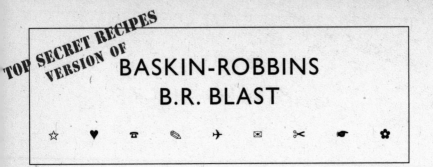

Burt Baskin and Irv Robbins' idea to franchise their ice cream stores for rapid growth was so inspired that the company's former milk shake machine salesman, Ray Kroc, adopted the technique to successfully expand his new chain of McDonald's hamburger outlets.

Ice cream is this chain's staple. So this coffee drink, unlike the Frappuccino made famous by Starbucks, requires adding ice cream for a creamy texture and rich taste. If you've got a blender you can clone either of the two varieties of this refreshing coffee beverage. For chocoholics bent on everything mocha, just add some chocolate syrup to the mix.

CAPPUCCINO

1 cup cold espresso or double-
   strength coffee (see Tidbits)
1 cup milk
⅓ cup granulated sugar
1 heaping cup vanilla ice cream

2 cups crushed ice or ice cubes

GARNISH
whipped cream
cinnamon

1. Combine the espresso, milk, and sugar in a blender and mix on medium speed for 15 seconds to dissolve sugar.
2. Add ice cream and ice, then blend on high speed until smooth and creamy.
3. Pour drink into two 16-ounce glasses. If desired, add whipped

cream to the top of each drink followed by a sprinkle of cinnamon.

- MAKES 2 LARGE DRINKS.

MOCHA

For this version, add 2 tablespoons of chocolate syrup to the recipe above and prepare as described.

TIDBITS

Make double-strength coffee in your coffee maker by adding half the water suggested by the manufacturer. Allow coffee to chill in the refrigerator before using it in this recipe.

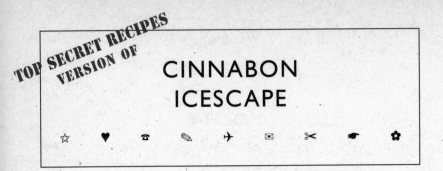

CINNABON ICESCAPE

☆ ♥ ☏ ✎ ✈ ✉ ✂ ☛ ✿

In a blender, Cinnabon adds concentrated flavoring, some ice and a curious secret ingredient referred to only as a "dairy product." When blended smooth, out come these thick, refreshing drinks that look and taste like they were made with ice cream. For this clone we just need a little half-and-half to give our version the exact same creamy consistency as the original with that custom "dairy" ingredient. Strawberry is the most popular of the flavors, but the other two are tasty as well. The Mochalatta version uses the *TSR* clone of the Mochalatta Chill (following this recipe on page 56) and produces a thicker blended version of the drink, similar to Starbucks' popular frozen Frappuccino.

STRAWBERRY

I cup water	½ cup half-and-half
¼ cup granulated sugar	¼ cup lemon juice
3 cups crushed ice	¼ cup Hershey's strawberry syrup
½ cup frozen whole strawberries (4 large strawberries)	

1. Combine the water and sugar in a cup and stir until the sugar is dissolved.
2. Combine this sugar syrup with remaining ingredients in a blender. Blend on high speed until the drink is smooth. Serve in two 16-ounce glasses.

• MAKES 2 LARGE DRINKS.

ORANGE

3 cups crushed ice
1 cup water
⅔ cup orange juice

½ cup half-and-half
3 tablespoons Tang orange drink
mix

Mix all ingredients in a blender set on high speed until smooth and creamy. Serve in two 16-ounce glasses.

- MAKES 2 LARGE DRINKS.

MOCHALATTA

3 cups crushed ice
1 ½ cups TSR version of
Mochalatta Chill (found on
page 56)

½ cup half-and-half
2 tablespoons chocolate syrup

Mix all ingredients in a blender set on high speed until smooth and creamy. Serve in two 16-ounce glasses.

- MAKES 2 LARGE DRINKS.

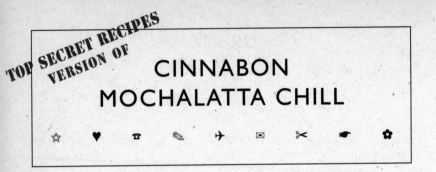

CINNABON MOCHALATTA CHILL

If you want your refreshing caffeine buzz kicked up with a nice chocolate rush, try this clone for Cinnabon's Mochalatta Chill. Brew some strong coffee and let it cool off, then get out the half-and-half and chocolate syrup. The real thing from Cinnabon is made with Ghirardelli chocolate syrup, but Hershey's syrup, which can be found everywhere, works great for this delicious duplicate.

1 cup double-strength coffee, cold **GARNISH**
   (see Tidbits) *whipped cream*
1 cup half-and-half
½ cup Hershey's chocolate syrup

Combine all ingredients in a small pitcher. Stir well or cover and shake. Pour over ice in two 16-ounce glasses, and top with whipped cream.

• MAKES 2 LARGE DRINKS.

TIDBITS

Make double-strength coffee in your coffee maker by adding half the water suggested by the manufacturer. Allow coffee to chill in the refrigerator before using it in this recipe.

It's Dairy Queen's most successful product ever. Over 175 million Blizzards were sold in the year following the product's debut in 1985. Such a sales phenomenon was the new creation that other fast food chains invented their own versions of the soft-serve ice cream treats with mixed in chunks of cookies and candies and fruit. McDonald's McFlurry is one popular example. Today there are over a dozen varieties of the frozen treat to choose from at Dairy Queen, and I've got all of the most creative and tasty versions cloned right here. Even though Oreo Cookie, Reese's Peanut Butter Cup, Butterfinger, and M&M's are four of the top five most-requested varieties at Dairy Queen, I've left those versions out of this section, and included them instead in the McFlurry clones on pages 65–67.

The biggest challenge we face when making our Blizzard replicas at home is keeping the ice cream from going all soft and runny on us when the other ingredients are stirred in. To solve that problem, we'll use a special technique inspired by marble slab ice cream stores. These outfits mix your choice of chunky ingredients with your choice of ice cream on a slab of frozen stone. This method keeps the ice cream cold and firm while mixing, until it's served to a drooling you.

To incorporate this technique at home you need to put a glass or ceramic bowl in the freezer for at least 30 minutes (while you're at it you may also want to freeze the glass you're going to serve the thing in). An hour or more is even better. Then, we simply mix our ingredients in the icy bowl, while the ice cream stays frosty cold. Just be sure to use plain vanilla ice cream (not French vanilla) for these clones, if you have a choice.

BABY RUTH

1 Baby Ruth candy bar
2½ cups vanilla ice cream

¼ cup milk
3 tablespoons caramel topping

1. Before you start to make this clone, freeze a medium glass or ceramic bowl in the freezer for at least 30 minutes.
2. When the bowl is frozen, mince the Baby Ruth into small bits with a big knife.
3. Measure the ice cream into the bowl, and add the milk. Stir the ice cream and milk together until smooth and creamy. Add the candy bar pieces and caramel and stir to combine. Pour into a 20-ounce glass and serve with a long spoon.

• MAKES 1 20-OUNCE SERVING.

BANANA PUDDING

Amaze everybody with this one that tastes just like homemade banana pudding with Nilla Wafers in it.

1 ripe banana
8 Nilla Wafers

2½ cups vanilla ice cream
¼ cup milk

1. Before you start to make this clone, freeze a medium glass or ceramic bowl in the freezer for at least 30 minutes.
2. Mash the banana in a separate small bowl.
3. Crumble the Nilla Wafers into small pieces.
4. Measure the ice cream and milk into the frozen bowl. Stir with a spoon until smooth and creamy.
5. Add the banana and Nilla Wafers to the ice cream and stir to combine.
6. Pour into a 20-ounce glass and serve with a long spoon.

• MAKES 1 20-OUNCE SERVING.

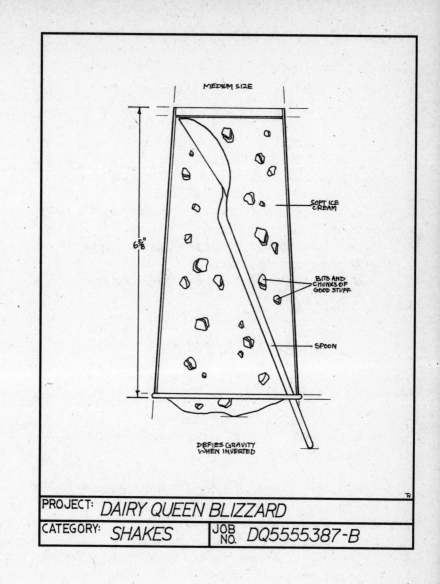

MEDIUM SIZE

SOFT ICE CREAM

BITS AND
CHUNKS OF
GOOD STUFF

SPOON

6⅝"

DEFIES GRAVITY
WHEN INVERTED

PROJECT: DAIRY QUEEN BLIZZARD		
CATEGORY: SHAKES	JOB NO.	DQ5555387-B

BANANA SPLIT

Tastes like a banana split with all the toppings. Yum city.

1 ripe banana
2½ cups vanilla ice cream
¼ cup milk

3 tablespoons strawberry topping
3 tablespoons pineapple topping
2 tablespoons chocolate syrup

1. Before you start to make this clone, freeze a medium glass or ceramic bowl in the freezer for at least 30 minutes.
2. Mash the banana in a separate small bowl.
3. Measure the ice cream and milk into the frozen bowl. Stir with a spoon until smooth and creamy.
4. Add the banana, strawberry topping, pineapple topping, and chocolate syrup and stir to combine.
5. Pour into a 20-ounce glass and serve with a long spoon.

- MAKES 1 20-OUNCE SERVING.

BERRY BANANA

With strawberry ice cream topping, banana, and crumbled Vienna Fingers you can't go wrong.

1 ripe banana
2 Vienna Fingers cookies
2½ cups vanilla ice cream

¼ cup milk
¼ cup strawberry topping

1. Before you start to make this clone, freeze a medium glass or ceramic bowl in the freezer for at least 30 minutes.
2. Mash the banana in a separate small bowl.
3. Crumble the Vienna Fingers into small pieces.
4. Measure the ice cream and milk into the frozen bowl. Stir with a spoon until smooth and creamy.
5. Add the banana, Vienna Fingers, and strawberries to the ice cream and stir to combine.
6. Pour into a 20-ounce glass and serve with a long spoon.

- MAKES 1 20-OUNCE SERVING.

CHOCOLATE CHIP

Use Magic Shell topping here, which will harden into little bits while mixing to create chocolate chips.

2½ cups vanilla ice cream   3 tablespoons chocolate Magic
¼ cup milk   Shell topping

1. Before you start to make this clone, freeze a medium glass or ceramic bowl in the freezer for at least 30 minutes.
2. Measure the ice cream and milk into the frozen bowl. Stir with a spoon until smooth and creamy.
3. Add the chocolate Magic Shell and stir gently to combine.
4. Pour into a 20-ounce glass and serve with a long spoon.

• MAKES 1 20-OUNCE SERVING.

CHOCOLATE CHIP COOKIE DOUGH

The dough comes from a tube of Pillsbury cookie dough. It's simple and sinfully good.

¼ cup Pillsbury cookie dough   ¼ cup milk
2½ cups vanilla ice cream   ¼ cup fudge topping

1. Before you start to make this clone, freeze a medium glass or ceramic bowl in the freezer for at least 30 minutes.
2. While the bowl is freezing, separate the cookie dough into pea-sized pieces and keep the dough pieces in the refrigerator.
3. Measure the ice cream and milk into the frozen bowl. Stir with a spoon until smooth and creamy.
4. Add the cookie dough and fudge topping and stir to combine.
5. Pour into a 20-ounce glass and serve with a long spoon.

• MAKES 1 20-OUNCE SERVING.

HAWAIIAN

If you like riding a wave of tropical flavors, you'll love this blend of pineapple ice cream topping and shredded coconut. Aloha, baby.

1 ripe banana
2½ cups vanilla ice cream
¼ cup milk

3 tablespoons pineapple topping
3 tablespoons shredded coconut ·

1. Before you start to make this clone, freeze a medium glass or ceramic bowl in the freezer for at least 30 minutes.
2. Mash the banana in a separate small bowl.
3. Measure the ice cream and milk into the frozen bowl. Stir with a spoon until smooth and creamy.
4. Add the mashed banana, pineapple topping, and coconut and stir to combine.
5. Pour into a 20-ounce glass and serve with a long spoon.

• MAKES 1 20-OUNCE SERVING.

WHOPP'N'WILD

You can't go wrong with a blend of Whoppers and ice cream. The flavor of malted milk ball candy is accentuated with the addition of extra malted milk powder and chocolate sauce.

16 Whoppers malted milk balls
2½ cups vanilla ice cream
¼ cup milk

2 tablespoons malted milk powder
3 tablespoons chocolate sauce

1. Before you start to make this clone, freeze a medium glass or ceramic bowl in the freezer for at least 30 minutes. While you're at it, put the Whoppers in a small plastic bag and put them in the freezer too.
2. When the bowl is frozen, remove the Whoppers from the freezer and, while they are still in the bag, smash them into pieces with your fist or the handle of a knife.

3. Measure the ice cream and milk into the frozen bowl. Stir with a spoon until smooth and creamy.
4. Add the Whoppers, malted milk powder, and chocolate sauce to the ice cream and stir to combine.
5. Pour into a 20-ounce glass and serve with a long spoon.

- MAKES 1 20-OUNCE SERVING.

YUKON CRUNCHER

Just like eating s'mores, except you use a spoon and this version is cold.

2½ cups vanilla ice cream
¼ cup milk
3 tablespoons fudge topping

3 tablespoons marshmallow
  crème
¼ cup Rice Krispies cereal

1. Before you start to make this clone, freeze a medium glass or ceramic bowl in the freezer for at least 30 minutes.
2. Measure the ice cream and milk into the frozen bowl. Stir with a spoon until smooth and creamy.
3. Add the fudge, marshmallow crème, and Rice Krispies to the ice cream and stir to combine.
4. Pour into a 20-ounce glass and serve with a long spoon.

- MAKES 1 20-OUNCE SERVING.

TIDBITS

If your Blizzard clone is not as thick as the real thing, just put the whole glass into the freezer for 5 to 10 minutes, or until it's thick.

JACK IN THE BOX
OREO COOKIE SHAKE

☆　♥　☎　✎　✈　⊠　✂　☞　❀

If you live in one of the 15 Western states served by Jack in the Box, you have no doubt cracked a gut from the hilarious TV ads produced by this popular hamburger chain. In the spots a suit-wearing "Jack" runs the company, even though he's got a bulbous antenna ball for a head with a smiley-face painted on it. He has a private jet, he plays golf, and he even has kids with mini antenna-ball heads.

Jack also has a featured shake flavor that, as it turns out, is very easy to make at home with a blender, ice cream, milk, and a handful of Oreo cookies. Sure, the drive-thru is convenient and easy. But if you don't feel like getting out, now you can enjoy this clone at home from the first fast food chain in the country to use a drive-thru window way back when.

3 cups vanilla ice cream   8 Oreo cookies
1 ½ cups milk

1. Combine the ice cream and milk in a blender and mix on low speed until smooth. Stir the shake with a spoon to mix, if necessary.
2. Break Oreo cookies while adding them to the blender. Mix on low speed for 5 to 10 seconds or until cookies are mostly pureed into the shake, but a few larger pieces remain. Stir with a spoon to help combine the cookies, if necessary.
3. Pour shake into two 12-ounce glasses.

• SERVES 2.

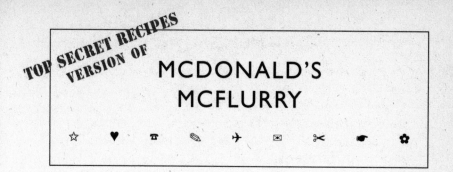

MCDONALD'S MCFLURRY

These 16-ounce desserts-in-a-cup are made with McDonald's soft-serve ice cream and one of several crumbled sweet additives. Duplicating soft-serve ice cream at home comes easy using regular vanilla ice cream (not French vanilla), a little whole milk, and a frozen bowl to do the mixing. You might also want to freeze the glass that you plan to serve this in to ensure the ice cream is served up creamy yet firm, rather than melted and soupy.

BUTTERFINGER

2 cups vanilla ice cream
1/4 cup milk

2/3 Butterfinger candy bar

1. Freeze a medium glass or ceramic bowl in the freezer for at least 30 minutes. Freeze the Butterfinger candy bar (in a plastic bag) as well, along with the 16-ounce glass you plan to use.
2. When the bowl is frozen, first break your candy bar (while it's still in the bag) into little pieces with the handle of a butter knife.
3. Pour the ice cream and milk into the frozen bowl and stir well until smooth and creamy.
4. Add the candy bar pieces and stir, then pour into the frozen 16-ounce glass and serve with a spoon.

• MAKES 1 16-OUNCE DESSERT.

M&M'S

2 cups vanilla ice cream
¼ cup milk

¼ cup (1 mega-tube) M&M's Minis

1. Freeze a medium glass or ceramic bowl in the freezer for at least 30 minutes. While you're at it put the 16-ounce glass you plan to use in there as well.
2. When the bowl is frozen, pour the ice cream and milk into the frozen bowl and stir well until smooth and creamy.
3. Add the M&M's and stir, then pour it all into the frozen 16-ounce glass and serve with a spoon.

• MAKES 1 16-OUNCE DESSERT.

OREO COOKIE

2 cups vanilla ice cream
¼ cup milk

3 Oreo cookies

1. Freeze a medium glass or ceramic bowl in the freezer for at least 30 minutes. While you're at it put the 16-ounce glass you plan to use in there as well.
2. When the bowl is frozen, crumble the cookies (in a plastic bag) into little pieces with your fist or the handle of a butter knife.
3. Pour the ice cream and milk into the frozen bowl and stir well until smooth and creamy.
4. Add the Oreo cookie pieces and stir, then pour it all into the frozen 16-ounce glass and serve with a spoon.

• MAKES 1 16-OUNCE DESSERT.

REESE'S

2 cups vanilla ice cream
¼ cup milk

2 Reese's Peanut Butter Cups (1 package)

1. Freeze a medium glass or ceramic bowl in the freezer for at least 30 minutes. Freeze the peanut butter cups in a plastic bag, and while you're at it put the 16-ounce glass you plan to use in there as well.
2. When the bowl is frozen, break the peanut butter cups (while still in the bag) into little pieces with the handle of a butter knife.
3. Pour the ice cream and milk into the frozen bowl and stir well until smooth and creamy.
4. Add the candy pieces and stir, then pour into the frozen 16-ounce glass and serve with a spoon.

- MAKES 1 16-OUNCE DESSERT.

MCDONALD'S
SHAKES

☆ ♥ ☎ ✎ ✈ ✉ ✂ ☞ ✿

Forty million customers get a dose of Mickey D's fast food every day. That also happens to be the exact same number of Americans who snore every night. Coincidence? But seriously, with all those daily McDonald's fans, you have to figure that at least a million or so go for one of the chain's three standard flavors of thick shakes: vanilla, chocolate, or strawberry (as for the special Shamrock Shake, we'll talk about that one in the next recipe). The clone recipes here are quick since each one requires just three simple ingredients and a blender to mix it all up. How McEasy is that? Throw everything in a blender and press a button—the one on the right. And if you want your shake thicker, just stash it in the freezer for a while.

CHOCOLATE SHAKE

2 cups vanilla ice cream
1 ¼ cups low-fat milk

2 tablespoons chocolate flavor
Nesquik mix

STRAWBERRY SHAKE

2 cups vanilla ice cream
1 ¼ cups low-fat milk

3 tablespoons strawberry flavor
Nesquik mix

VANILLA SHAKE

2 cups vanilla ice cream   *3 tablespoons sugar*
1 ¼ cups low-fat milk

1. Combine all ingredients for the shake flavor of your choice in a blender and mix on high speed until smooth. Stop blender, stir if necessary, and blend again to help combine the ingredients.
2. Pour into two 12-ounce cups.

• SERVES 2.

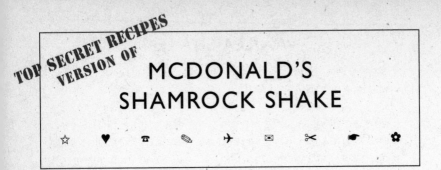

MCDONALD'S SHAMROCK SHAKE

You'll find it very easy to re-create the flavors of McDonald's perennial St. Patrick's Day shake using only four ingredients. The two that make this holiday shake unique are the mint extract and green food coloring. Make sure your extract says "mint" and not "peppermint." And if you don't want shakes that are green like the real ones, you can certainly leave out the food coloring. After all, it's only for looks. Now you can sip on a Shamrock any time of the year. Blarney!

2 cups vanilla ice cream
1 1/4 cups low-fat milk

1/4 teaspoon mint extract (not peppermint)
8 drops green food coloring

1. Combine all ingredients in a blender and blend on high speed until smooth. Stop blender to stir with a spoon if necessary to help blend ice cream.
2. Pour into two 12-ounce cups and serve each with a straw.

• SERVES 2.

SONIC DRIVE-IN CREAM PIE SHAKES

☆ ♥ ☎ ✎ ✈ ✉ ✄ ☛ ✿

If you placed all the cups end to end that Sonic uses in a year, they would circle the earth twice. That's including the detour the cups would make to avoid passing through downtown Detroit.

These awesome shakes are unique for the graham cracker crumbs in the mix that make them taste as if you're slurping up a creamy chilled pie. You can either crumble up your own graham crackers or use the already ground stuff in a box that's used most often to make graham cracker pie crusts.

BANANA

If you love banana cream pies, you'll love this shake. Just be sure your banana is ripe.

2½ cups vanilla ice cream
½ cup milk
1 ripe banana
2 tablespoons graham cracker
   crumbs

GARNISH
whipped cream
graham cracker crumbs

1. Put all ingredients in a blender and mix until smooth. You may have to stop the blender and stir the shake with a spoon so that it blends evenly.
2. Pour the shake into two 12-ounce glasses. Garnish each serv-

ing with a dollop of whipped cream, and shake some graham cracker crumbs over the top. Serve with a straw.

- MAKES 2 12-OUNCE SHAKES.

CHOCOLATE

Simply add a little chocolate syrup to the shake if chocolate is your thing. This recipe makes two medium shakes or one big one for real chocoholics.

2½ cups vanilla ice cream
½ cup milk
2 tablespoons Hershey's
    chocolate syrup
2 tablespoons graham cracker
    crumbs

GARNISH
whipped cream
graham cracker crumbs

1. Put all ingredients in a blender and mix until smooth. You may have to stop the blender and stir the shake with a spoon so that it blends evenly.
2. Pour the shake into two 12-ounce glasses. Garnish each serving with a dollop of whipped cream, and shake some graham cracker crumbs over the top. Serve with a straw.

- MAKES 2 12-OUNCE SHAKES.

COCONUT

This shake uses cream of coconut for flavoring. This is the canned ingredient used most often to make pina coladas, and can be found near the bar mixers in your supermarket.

2½ cups vanilla ice cream
½ cup milk
¼ cup cream of coconut
2 tablespoons graham cracker
    crumbs

GARNISH
whipped cream
graham cracker crumbs

1. Put all ingredients in a blender and mix until smooth. You may have to stop the blender and stir the shake with a spoon so that it blends evenly.
2. Pour the shake into two 12-ounce glasses. Garnish each serving with a dollop of whipped cream, and shake some graham cracker crumbs over the top. Serve with a straw.

• MAKES 2 12-OUNCE SHAKES.

STRAWBERRY

This flavor uses the frozen sliced strawberries that are found in boxes in the freezer section with the other frozen fruit. Thaw out a box and measure the berries along with the syrup into the blender.

2½ cups vanilla ice cream
½ cup milk
¼ cup frozen sweetened sliced
   strawberries, thawed
2 tablespoons graham cracker
   crumbs

GARNISH
whipped cream
graham cracker crumbs

1. Put all ingredients in a blender and mix until smooth. You may have to stop the blender and stir the shake with a spoon so that it blends evenly.
2. Pour the shake into two 12-ounce glasses. Garnish each serving with a dollop of whipped cream, and shake some graham cracker crumbs over the top. Serve with a straw.

• MAKES 2 12-OUNCE SHAKES.

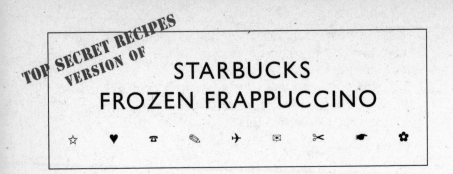

STARBUCKS FROZEN FRAPPUCCINO

It was in 1995 that Starbucks stores started selling this frozen drink, one of the company's most successful new products. The Frappuccino is blended with strong coffee, sugar, a dairy base, and ice. Each one is made to order and each one is guaranteed to give you a throbbing brain freeze if you sip too hard. The drinks come in several different varieties, the most popular of which I've cloned here for your frontal lobe—pounding, caffeine-buzzing pleasure.

Make double-strength coffee by measuring 2 tablespoons of ground coffee per cup (serving) in your coffee maker. The drink will be even more authentic if you use Starbucks beans and grind them yourself just before brewing.

COFFEE

¾ cup double-strength coffee, cold
1 cup low-fat milk

3 tablespoons granulated sugar
2 cups ice

1. Make double-strength coffee by brewing with twice the coffee required by your coffee maker. That should be 2 tablespoons of ground coffee per each cup of coffee. Chill before using.
2. To make drink, combine all ingredients in a blender and blend on high speed until ice is crushed and drink is smooth. Pour into two 16-ounce glasses, and serve with a straw.

- MAKES 2 "GRANDE" DRINKS.

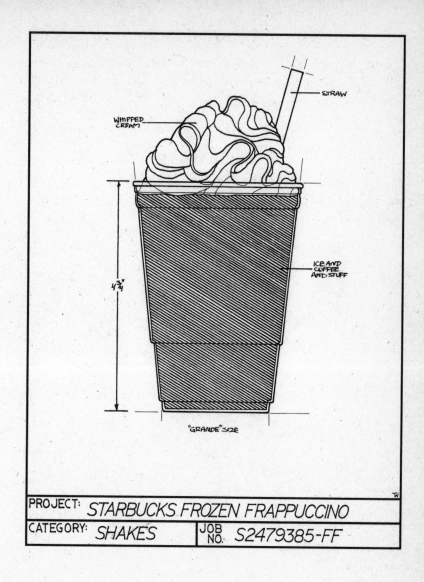

STRAW

WHIPPED
CREAM

ICE AND
COFFEE
AND STUFF

4¾"

"GRANDE" SIZE

Ͳ

PROJECT: *STARBUCKS FROZEN FRAPPUCCINO*

CATEGORY: *SHAKES*   JOB NO. *S2479385-FF*

CARAMEL

For this version, add 3 tablespoons of caramel topping to the original recipe and prepare as described. Top each glass with whipped cream and drizzle additional caramel over the whipped cream.

MOCHA

For this version, add 3 tablespoons Hershey's chocolate syrup to the original recipe and prepare as described. Top each glass with whipped cream, if desired.

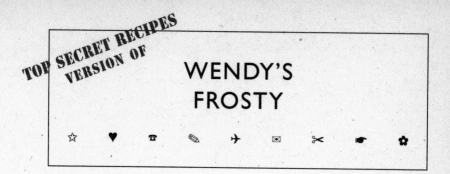

WENDY'S
FROSTY

☆   ♥   ☎   ✎   ✈   ✉   ✂   ☞   ✿

First served at Wendy's in 1969, the Frosty continues as a favorite in fast food shakes, even if it only comes in chocolate flavor. This clone recipe is an improved version of the recipe that appears in the first book, *Top Secret Recipes*. I've designed this for just a one-person serving and have reduced the chocolate in the shake so that it's more like the real thing served today. I find the smaller yield also helps to make the thing blend better.

½ cup milk   2 cups vanilla ice cream
4 teaspoons Nesquik chocolate
   drink mix

Combine all of the ingredients in a blender. Blend on medium speed, stopping to stir several times with a long spoon, if necessary, to help the ingredients blend well.

• MAKES 1 SERVING.

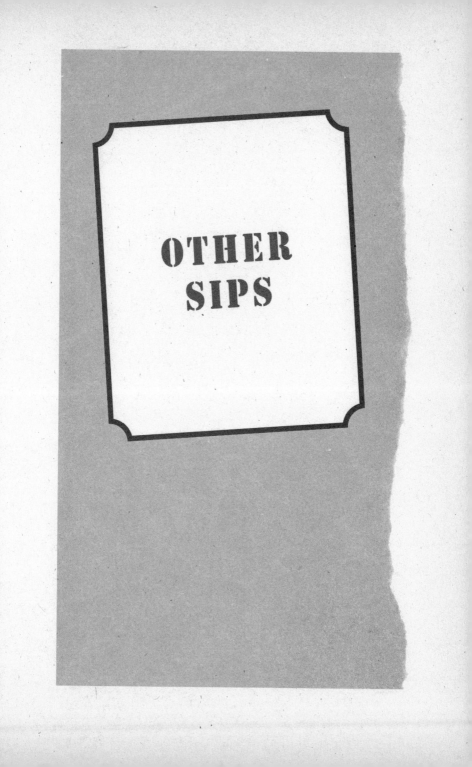

OTHER
SIPS

ARIZONA GREEN TEA WITH GINSENG AND HONEY

Hard to believe it takes only one regular-sized green tea bag to make an entire 2-quart clone of the popular iced tea in the foam green bottles. Ah, but it's true. Find the liquid ginseng for this recipe in your local health food store, and try to get American ginseng if you can because the Chinese stuff tastes kinda nasty.

2 quarts (8 cups) water
1 Lipton green tea bag
½ cup sugar
2 tablespoons honey

3 tablespoons lemon juice
¼ teaspoon ginseng extract
   (American ginseng)

1. Heat water in a large saucepan until it boils. Turn off heat, put the teabag in the water, then cover the pan and let the tea steep for 1 hour.
2. Pour the sugar and honey into a 2-quart pitcher. Pour the tea into the pitcher and stir to dissolve sugar.
3. Add lemon juice and ginseng and stir. Cool and serve.

• MAKES 2 QUARTS.

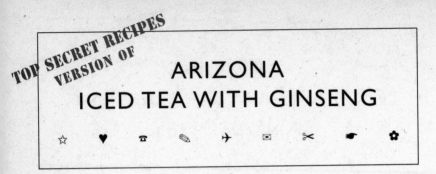

ARIZONA
ICED TEA WITH GINSENG

When John Ferolito and Don Vultaggio pondered a name for a new line of canned iced teas, all they had to do was look at a map of the United States. They wanted to name their iced tea after a hot place where a cold can of iced tea was worshipped. Originally they picked "Santa Fe," but soon ditched the name of the city and settled on a state: AriZona, complete with an uppercase "Z" in the middle for kicks. The secret to the duo's early success was largely in their creative packaging decisions. If you think the tea's great chilled, the company claims you can also sip it hot by simply zapping a cupful in the microwave.

2 quarts (8 cups) water
1 Lipton tea bag (black tea)
⅔ cup sugar

2 tablespoons lemon juice
¼ teaspoon ginseng extract
   (American ginseng)

1. Heat water in a large saucepan until it boils. Turn off heat, put the teabag in the water, then cover the pan and let the tea steep for 1 hour.
2. Pour the sugar into a 2-quart pitcher. Pour the tea into the pitcher and stir to dissolve sugar.
3. Add lemon juice and ginseng and stir. Cool and serve.

• MAKES 2 QUARTS.

You can find liquid ginseng, usually in dropper bottles, in your local health food store. Be sure to get American ginseng if you have a choice. Some of the Chinese ginseng tastes too bitter for this tea.

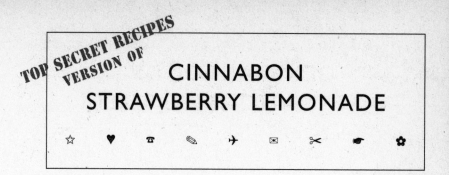

CINNABON
STRAWBERRY LEMONADE

☆ ♥ ☎ ✎ ✈ ✉ ✂ ☞ ✿

Cinnabon, the 470-unit chain famous for its gooey cinnamon rolls, gives lemonade a twist by adding strawberry syrup. It's a simple clone when you snag some Hershey's strawberry syrup (near the chocolate syrup in your supermarket), and a few juicy lemons. While you're at it, toss in a straw.

½ cup lemon juice (from 3 or 4
   fresh lemons)
¼ cup sugar

2 cups water
2 tablespoons Hershey's
   strawberry syrup

Mix ingredients together in a pitcher. Serve over ice with a straw, if you've got one.

• MAKES 2 DRINKS.

GENERAL FOODS INTERNATIONAL COFFEES

☆ ♥ ☎ ✎ ✈ ✉ ✂ ☞ ✿

With just a few simple ingredients you can re-create the European-style coffees that come in rectangular tins at a fraction of the cost. Since these famous instant coffee blends are created by Maxwell House, it's best to use Maxwell House instant coffee, although I've tried them all with Folgers and Taster's Choice, and the recipes still work out fine. You'll also need a coffee bean grinder to grind the instant coffee into powder. When you're finished making the mix, you can store it for as long as you like in a sealed container, until you're ready for a hot coffee drink. At that point, simply measure some of the mix into a cup with boiling water. Stir it all up and enjoy while watching shows about Europe on the Travel Channel to enhance the experience.

CAFÉ VIENNA

A creamy coffee with a hint of cinnamon.

¼ cup instant coffee
¼ cup plus 3 tablespoons
    granulated sugar

½ cup plus 1 tablespoon
    Coffee-mate creamer
⅛ teaspoon cinnamon

1. Grind the instant coffee into powder using a coffee grinder.
2. Mix all ingredients together in a small bowl. Store in a sealed container.
3. To make coffee, measure 2 tablespoons of the powdered mix

into a coffee cup. Add 8 ounces (1 cup) of boiling water and stir.

- MAKES 9 SERVINGS.

FRENCH VANILLA CAFÉ

This one gets its subtle vanilla flavor from a little French Vanilla Coffee-mate creamer.

¼ cup instant coffee
¼ cup plus 3 tablespoons
  granulated sugar

½ cup Coffee-mate creamer
  (plain)
¼ cup French Vanilla Coffee-mate
  creamer

1. Grind the instant coffee into powder using a coffee grinder.
2. Mix all ingredients together in a small bowl. Store in a sealed container.
3. To make coffee, measure 2 tablespoons of the powdered mix into a coffee cup. Add 8 ounces (1 cup) of boiling water and stir.

- MAKES 10 SERVINGS.

HAZELNUT BELGIAN CAFÉ

As in the above recipe, you'll need to use flavored creamer along with the plain stuff to hit the right note.

¼ cup instant coffee
¼ cup plus 3 tablespoons
  granulated sugar
¼ cup plus 3 tablespoons Coffee-
  mate creamer (plain)

2 tablespoons Hazelnut
  Coffee-mate creamer

1. Grind the instant coffee into powder using a coffee grinder.
2. Mix all ingredients together in a small bowl. Store in a sealed container.
3. To make coffee, measure 2 tablespoons of the powdered mix

into a coffee cup. Add 8 ounces (1 cup) of boiling water and stir.

- MAKES 9 SERVINGS.

SUISSE MOCHA

It takes just a couple tablespoons of cocoa to give this version its chocolate accent. When making the coffee in a cup, notice that this is the only recipe of the bunch requiring a measurement of 4 teaspoons of mix to 1 cup of boiling water.

¼ cup instant coffee
½ cup plus 2 tablespoons
  granulated sugar

½ cup plus 1 tablespoon Coffee-mate creamer
2 tablespoons cocoa

1. Grind the instant coffee into powder using a coffee grinder.
2. Mix all ingredients together in a small bowl. Store in a sealed container.
3. To make coffee, measure 4 teaspoons of the powdered mix into a coffee cup. Add 8 ounces (1 cup) of boiling water and stir.

- MAKES 16 SERVINGS.

VIENNESE CHOCOLATE CAFÉ

Vanilla and chocolate go great together in this one.

¼ cup instant coffee
¼ cup plus 3 tablespoons
  granulated sugar
½ cup Coffee-mate creamer
  (plain)

2 tablespoons French Vanilla
  Coffee-mate creamer
2 teaspoons cocoa

1. Grind the instant coffee into powder using a coffee grinder.
2. Mix all ingredients together in a small bowl. Store in a sealed container.
3. To make coffee, measure 2 tablespoons of the powdered mix into a coffee cup. Add 8 ounces (1 cup) of boiling water and stir.

- MAKES 10 SERVINGS.

HAWAIIAN PUNCH
FRUIT JUICY RED

☆　♥　☎　✎　✈　✉　✂　☛　✿

Real Hawaiian Punch contains only 5 percent fruit juice. Even though some of the ingredients in our clone are not pure fruit juice, and we're adding additional water and sugar, this *Top Secret Recipes* version still contains a lot more tasty real fruit juice than the real thing. Plus, you can leave the food coloring out, if you like. It's only for looks, in a traditionally punchy way.

1 ½ cups water
1 cup pineapple juice
¾ cup Mauna Lai Paradise
   Passion guava/passion fruit
   blend
¼ tablespoon orange juice

¼ cup apple juice
¼ cup Kern's papaya nectar
¼ tablespoon Kern's apricot
   nectar
3 tablespoons granulated sugar
¼ teaspoon red food coloring

Combine all ingredients in a pitcher and stir until sugar is dissolved.

• MAKES 1 LITER.

HOT DOG ON A STICK
MUSCLE BEACH LEMONADE

☆   ♥   ☎   ✎   ✈   ⊠   ✂   ☞   ✿

Entrepreneur Dave Barham opened the first Hot Dog on a Stick location in Santa Monica, California, near famed Muscle Beach. That was in 1946, and today the chain has blossomed into a total of more than 100 outlets located in shopping malls across America. You've probably seen the bright red, white, blue, and yellow go-go outfits and those cylindrical fez-style bucket hats on the girls behind the counter.

In giant clear plastic vats at the front of each store floats ice, fresh lemon rinds, and what is probably the world's most thirst-quenching substance—Muscle Beach Lemonade. Our clone is a simple concoction really, with only three ingredients. And with this *TSR* formula, you'll have your own version of the lemonade in the comfort of your own home at a fraction of the price.

1 cup fresh-squeezed lemon juice (about 5 lemons)	7 cups water
	1 cup granulated sugar

1. Combine the lemon juice with the water and sugar in a 2-quart pitcher. Stir or shake vigorously until all the sugar is dissolved.
2. Slice the remaining lemon rind halves into fourths, then add the rinds to the pitcher. Add ice to the top of the pitcher and chill.
3. Serve the lemonade over ice in a 12-ounce glass and add a couple of lemon rind slices to each glass.

• MAKES 2 QUARTS, OR 8 SERVINGS.

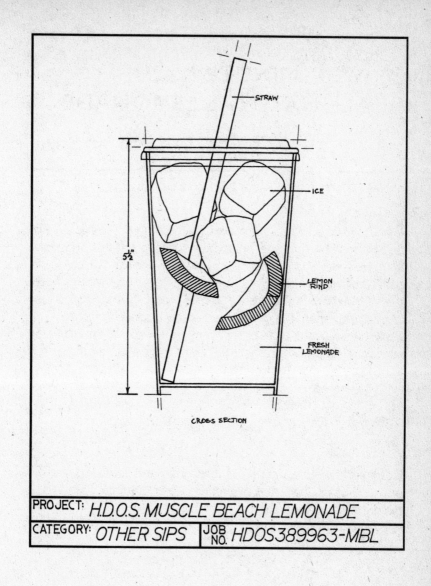

STRAW

ICE

LEMON RIND

FRESH LEMONADE

$5\frac{1}{2}"$

CROSS SECTION

PROJECT:	*H.D.O.S. MUSCLE BEACH LEMONADE*	
CATEGORY: *OTHER SIPS*	JOB NO.	*HDOS389963-MBL*

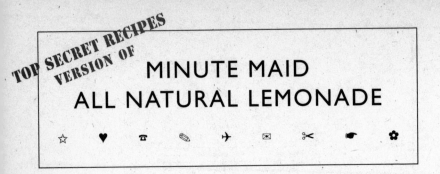

MINUTE MAID
ALL NATURAL LEMONADE

Minute Maid is credited with creating the modern orange juice industry by marketing the first frozen concentrated orange juice in 1946. Today the company is owned by The Coca-Cola Company and sells juices, punches, and fruit drinks in countries all over the world. Minute Maid also sells one of the most recognized brands of lemonade, made from lemon concentrate. You can easily duplicate the taste of the drink at home, but since this *TSR* version is made with fresh lemons, it might just edge out the real thing in a side-by-side taste test.

½ cup fresh-squeezed lemon juice
   (from 2 to 3 lemons)
3¼ cups water

¼ cup plus 3 tablespoons
   granulated sugar

Combine the lemon juice with the water and sugar in a 1-quart pitcher. Stir or shake the pitcher vigorously until all the sugar is dissolved. Cover and chill.

• MAKES 1 QUART.

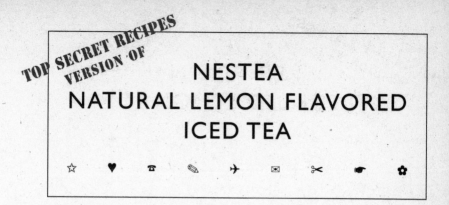

NESTEA
NATURAL LEMON FLAVORED
ICED TEA

☆   ♥   ☎   ✎   ✈   ✉   ✂   ☞   ✿

For five thousand years tea was served hot. But when a heat wave hit the World's Fair in St. Louis in 1904, tea plantation owner Richard Blechynden couldn't give the steamy stuff away. So he poured it over ice, creating the first iced tea, and the drink became the hit of the fair. Today Nestle's drink division, which markets Nestea, produces somewhere in the area of 50 percent of the world's processed tea. That's huge business when you consider that tea is second only to water in worldwide consumption.

2 quarts (8 cups) water
2 Lipton tea bags

¾ cup plus 2 tablespoons
granulated sugar
¼ cup bottled lemon juice

1. Bring 2 quarts of water to a boil. Add tea bags and let the tea steep for 1 to 2 hours.
2. Remove the tea bags and pour the tea into a 2-quart pitcher. Add sugar and lemon juice. Cover and chill.

- MAKES 2 QUARTS.

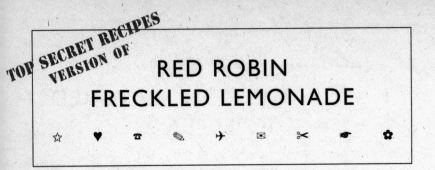

RED ROBIN
FRECKLED LEMONADE

This is Red Robin's signature non-alcoholic drink, and is simple to make with pre-made lemonade (unless you want to use one of the fresh lemonade recipes from page 88 or 90) and the strawberries that come frozen in sweet syrup. When added to the top of the ice-filled lemonade glass the strawberries and syrup speckle the drink. Serve this one without stirring it up, or the freckles will be gone.

⅓ cup frozen sweetened sliced
   strawberries, thawed
1 cup lemonade

GARNISH
lemon wedge

1. Fill a 16-ounce glass with ice.
2. Ladle strawberries with syrup over the top of the ice.
3. Fill the glass with lemonade. Add a lemon wedge and serve with a straw.

• MAKES 1 DRINK.

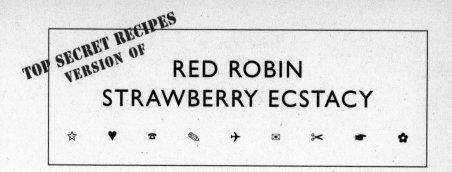

RED ROBIN
STRAWBERRY ECSTACY

☆   ♥   ☎   ✎   ✈   ✉   ✂   ☞   ✿

After adding the juices to the blender the restaurant does a "flash blend." That means you use just a couple of pulses on high speed so that the ice is broken up into small pieces, without being completely crushed to a slushy consistency.

½ cup orange juice
⅓ cup pineapple juice
½ ounce grenadine

1 cup ice
⅓ cup frozen sweetened sliced
    strawberries, thawed

1. Add orange juice, pineapple juice, grenadine, and ice to a blender. Blend the drink with just a couple pulses on high speed so that the ice is still a bit chunky.
2. Pour into a 16-ounce glass and ladle strawberries with the syrup into the drink.
3. Add a wedge of orange and a maraschino cherry speared on a toothpick. Serve with a straw.

• MAKES 1 DRINK.

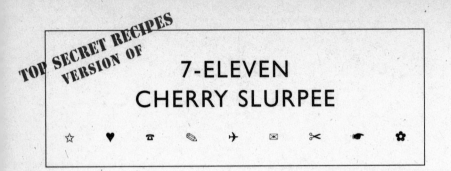

7-ELEVEN
CHERRY SLURPEE

☆　♥　☎　✎　✈　✉　✂　☛　✿

Put on a big red smile. Now you can make your own version of the popular convenience store slush we know by the excruciating brain throb that follows a big ol' gulp. You must have a blender to make this clone of 7-Eleven's Slurpee, and enough room to stick that blender into your freezer to get it nice and thick. This recipe gets close to the original with Kool-Aid mix and a little help from cherry extract, but you can make this drink with any flavor Kool-Aid mix (if you decide to make some variations, don't worry about adding extract). This recipe makes enough to fill one of those giant 32-ounce cups you find at the convenience store. Now if we could just figure out how to make those funky spoon-straws.

2 cups cold club soda
½ cup sugar
¼ teaspoon plus ⅛ teaspoon
  Kool-Aid cherry-flavored
  unsweetened drink mix

½ teaspoon cherry extract
2½ cups crushed ice

1. Pour 1 cup of the club soda into a blender. Add the sugar, Kool-Aid mix, and cherry extract. Blend this until all of the sugar is dissolved.
2. Add the crushed ice and blend on high speed until the drink is a slushy, smooth consistency, with no remaining chunks of ice.
3. Add the remaining club soda and blend briefly until mixed. You may have to stop the blender and use a long spoon to stir up the contents.

4. If necessary, put the blender into your freezer for ½ hour. This will help thicken it up. After ½ hour remove blender from freezer and, again, blend briefly to mix.

• MAKES 1 32-OUNCE DRINK (OR 2 16-OUNCERS).

SNAPPLE
ICED TEA

☆ ♥ ☎ ✎ ✈ ✉ ✂ ☞ ✿

Snapple was selling juices for five years—since 1982—before the fruity line of teas was rolled out. Just five years after that, Snapple was selling more tea in the U.S. than Lipton or Nestea. Today, even though Snapple sells over 50 different bottled beverages, the iced teas are still the most successful products in the line. But not all the fruity flavors of tea were hits. Cranberry, strawberry, and orange are now extinct, so those flavors can only be enjoyed by making versions of your own at home with these simple formulas. I've also got lemon and peach flavors here, Snapple's two top-selling products, plus raspberry, another big seller.

Included here are improved versions of iced tea clones printed in the book *More Top Secret Recipes*.

CRANBERRY ICED TEA

2 quarts (8 cups) water
2 Lipton tea bags
¾ cup granulated sugar

⅓ cup plus 2 tablespoons bottled lemon juice
2 tablespoons Ocean Spray cranberry juice cocktail concentrate

DIET LEMON ICED TEA

2 quarts (8 cups) water
2 Lipton tea bags
16 1-gram packages Equal sweetener

⅓ cup bottled lemon juice

LEMON ICED TEA

2 quarts (8 cups) water
2 Lipton tea bags

¾ cup granulated sugar
⅓ cup bottled lemon juice

ORANGE ICED TEA

2 quarts (8 cups) water
2 Lipton tea bags
¾ cup granulated sugar

⅓ cup bottled lemon juice
⅛ teaspoon orange extract

PEACH ICED TEA

2 quarts (8 cups) water
2 Lipton tea bags
¾ cup granulated sugar

¼ cup plus 1 tablespoon bottled
    lemon juice
3 tablespoons Torani peach
    flavoring syrup

Alternate clone: Rather than Torani peach flavoring use one 12-ounce can Kern's peach nectar, and 3 tablespoons lemon juice instead of ¼ cup plus 1 tablespoon lemon juice.

RASPBERRY ICED TEA

2 quarts (8 cups) water
2 Lipton tea bags
¾ cup granulated sugar

¼ cup plus 1 tablespoon lemon
    juice
2 tablespoons Torani raspberry
    flavoring syrup

STRAWBERRY ICED TEA

2 quarts (8 cups) water
2 Lipton tea bags
¾ cup granulated sugar

⅓ cup lemon juice
1 tablespoon strawberry extract

1. Bring water to a rapid boil in a large saucepan.
2. Turn off heat, add tea bags, cover saucepan and let the tea steep for 1 to 2 hours.
3. Pour the sugar into a 2-quart pitcher, and then add the tea. The water will still be warm and the sugar (or sweetener if making the diet tea) should dissolve easily.
4. Add the lemon juice and fruit flavoring ingredients. Stir, cover and chill.

- MAKES 2 QUARTS.

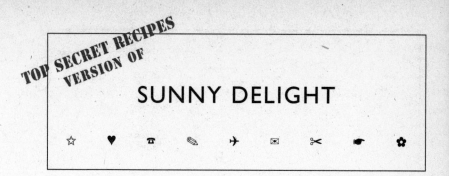

SUNNY DELIGHT

☆　♥　☎　✎　✈　✉　✂　☞　✿

If you love the taste of Sunny D but wish it was made with more than just 5 percent real fruit juice, this is the recipe for you. Rustle up some frozen juice concentrates and let them thaw out before measuring. Since tangerine juice concentrate is tough to find on its own I designed the recipe to use the orange tangerine blend concentrate from Minute Maid.

6 cups water
1 cup corn syrup
1 ⅓ cups frozen concentrated
　Minute Maid orange tangerine
　juice, thawed
6 tablespoons frozen concentra-
　ted apple juice, thawed

2 tablespoons frozen
　concentrated limeade, thawed
4 teaspoons frozen concentrated
　grapefruit juice, thawed
1 teaspoon Kool-Aid lemonade
　unsweetened drink mix

1. Combine all ingredients in a 2-quart pitcher. Stir well.
2. Chill for several hours before serving.

• MAKES 2 QUARTS.

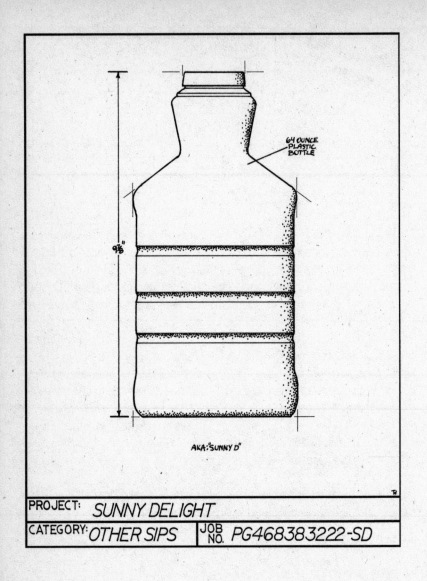

64 OUNCE
PLASTIC
BOTTLE

9⅝"

AKA:"SUNNY D"

PROJECT: *SUNNY DELIGHT*

CATEGORY: *OTHER SIPS*   JOB NO. *PG468383222-SD*

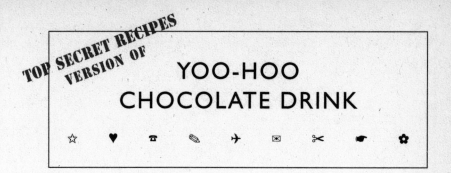

YOO-HOO CHOCOLATE DRINK

Watching his wife can tomatoes inspired Natale Olivieri to create a bottled chocolate drink with a long shelf life back in the early 1920s. When New York Yankee great Yogi Berra later met Natale and tasted his drink, he was an instant fan, and went on to help raise the funds that helped make Yoo-hoo a national success.

I cloned this drink in the first book, *Top Secret Recipes*, but have since discovered an improved technique. Using a blender to mix the drink, as instructed in that version, adds too much unnecessary foam. So here now is a revised recipe that you shake to mix, that could fool even the most devoted Yoo-hoo fanatics.

¾ cup nonfat dry milk
3 tablespoons Nesquik chocolate
  drink mix

1 ½ cups cold water

Combine all ingredients in a container or jar with a lid. Shake until dry milk is dissolved. Drink immediately or chill in refrigerator.

• MAKES 1 14-OUNCE DRINK.

YOO-HOO MIX-UPS

A while back when I was rummaging through my pantry I came upon several bottles of flavored Yoo-hoo that I'd scored from Wal-Mart and tucked away for over a year. Each of the bottles was covered with a little dust and needed a pretty fierce shaking, but the contents were very well preserved and quite tasty. After some web browsing of a few unofficial Yoo-hoo web sites, I discovered these previously worshipped "Mix-Ups" varieties of the famous chocolate drink had since been put to rest. Now, after a little work in the top secret underground lab, I've come up with a way to clone the flavor of this "dead product" that's no longer obtainable outside of the ethereal food-world afterlife.

CHOCOLATE-BANANA

¾ cup nonfat dry milk
3 tablespoons Nesquik chocolate
  drink mix

1½ cups cold water
1½ teaspoons sugar
½ teaspoon banana extract

CHOCOLATE-MINT

¾ cup nonfat dry milk
3 tablespoons Nesquik chocolate
  drink mix
1½ cups cold water

1 teaspoon sugar
dash mint extract (less than
  ⅛ teaspoon)

CHOCOLATE-STRAWBERRY

¾ cup nonfat dry milk
3 tablespoons Nesquik chocolate
   drink mix

1½ cups cold water
1 tablespoon sugar
1½ teaspoons strawberry extract

Combine all ingredients for flavor of your choice in a container or jar with a lid. Shake until dry milk is dissolved. Drink immediately or chill in refrigerator.

- MAKES 1 14-OUNCE DRINK.

SPIRITS:
Schnapps
& Liqueurs

Liqueur-making dates back to somewhere around 900 A.D., when Arabs and European monks had to do something to break up the boredom of living in 900 A.D. Think about it: no DVDs, no video games, no extreme sports on ESPN2. These guys had nothing better to do than spend their time crafting the perfect beverage on which to get wasted. I respectfully toast their devotion.

Luckily for us, creating liqueurs at home today is a much simpler task than in those days thanks to the availability of a variety of extracts and flavorings, and pre-distilled spirits. This leaves us plenty of time in one day to both make liqueur *and* watch a DVD.

These clone recipes are very easy. For most of them it's a simple matter of creating a simple syrup, then adding 80-proof vodka and the correct flavoring. Vodka works well because of its neutral flavor. You can use any inexpensive vodka you like, but I recommend Smirnoff. That's the brand I used to make these clones, since it tastes good without being too expensive. For the flavorings and extracts, try to use Schilling or McCormick brand.

Each of the recipes has been designed to create a finished product with the same approximate alcohol content as the original.

For the liqueurs with fruit additives or cocoa you will want to strain the liqueur to remove the sediment. For this, use a wire strainer that has been lined with a coffee filter or two, or a paper towel. Moisten the filters with a bit of water first, then, after the liqueur has aged a while, pour it in and let it drip through the filter. If the liqueur has settled for several days the sediment will be on the bottom of your bottle or jar, so if you pour carefully most of the solid material will stay behind. It may take several hours for all of the liqueur to drip through the filter.

Store your finished product in a tightly sealed bottle in a cool, dry place. Except for the Irish cream clone, your finished product will store indefinitely, and even improve with age.

Then go watch that DVD.

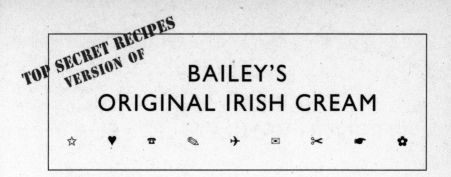

BAILEY'S ORIGINAL IRISH CREAM

☆ ♥ ☎ ✎ ✈ ⊠ ✄ ☞ ✿

Bailey's uses a special process to combine two otherwise incompatible ingredients: cream and whiskey. This secret process keeps the cream from clumping and separating from the whiskey, and allows the liqueur to go for two years unrefrigerated without spoiling. Since we can't use the same process, we'll replace cream with canned evaporated milk in our recipe. This gives us a finished product with the taste and texture of the deliciously famous Irish cream. Here now is an improved version of the Bailey's clone recipe that appears in *More Top Secret Recipes*. This version has fewer ingredients, is easier to make, and tastes amazing.

1½ cups evaporated milk
 (1 12-ounce can)
1 cup Irish whiskey
⅔ cup granulated sugar

1 tablespoon Hershey's chocolate
 syrup
1 teaspoon vanilla extract
½ teaspoon instant coffee

Combine all ingredients in a pitcher and mix well or shake until sugar is dissolved. Store in the refrigerator in a sealed container. Shake before serving.

- MAKES 3 CUPS.

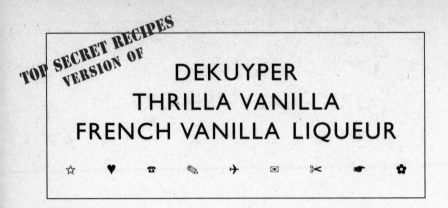

DEKUYPER
THRILLA VANILLA
FRENCH VANILLA LIQUEUR

☆　♥　☎　✎　✈　✉　✂　☛　✿

Just as with the real thing, this clone of the unique vanilla liqueur from DeKuyper can be mixed with cola over ice, or with 1 part vanilla liqueur to 2 parts raspberry liqueur for another tasty tipple. Also try splashing some of it into the shaker with your favorite vodka for a sweet vanilla-tini.

1 ¼ cups very hot water
¾ cup granulated sugar
1 cup 80-proof vodka

1 teaspoon McCormick vanilla
butter & nut flavoring

1. Dissolve sugar in the hot water.
2. Add vodka and flavoring, and stir well. Store in a sealed container.

• MAKES 2⅔ CUPS.

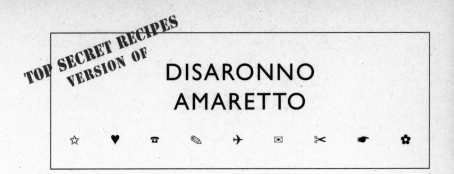

DISARONNO AMARETTO

☆ ♥ ☎ ✎ ✈ ⊠ ✄ ☛ ✿

The story behind this one is that for several months artist Bernardino Luini worked closely with a model to help him paint a fresco of the Madonna in Saronno, Italy. As the months passed the girl, whose name has since been forgotten, fell in love with Bernardino. To show her feelings for him, the girl gave Bernardino a gift of sweet almond-flavored liqueur she made from the trees growing in her garden. The year was 1525, and that bottle is said to have been the first DiSaronno Amaretto. The recipe was passed down through the ages, until late in the eighteenth century when the liqueur went into commercial production.

Reenact the legend by giving someone a bottle of your own version of the famous liqueur, whether they paint you on a wall or not.

½ cup granulated sugar
¼ cup dark brown sugar
¾ cup very hot water
½ cup corn syrup

1½ cups 80-proof vodka
1 tablespoon almond extract
1 teaspoon vanilla extract

1. Combine the water with the sugars in a medium glass pitcher or bowl. Stir until the sugar is dissolved. Add corn syrup and stir well.
2. Add vodka and flavorings and stir well. Store in a sealed container.

• MAKES 3 CUPS.

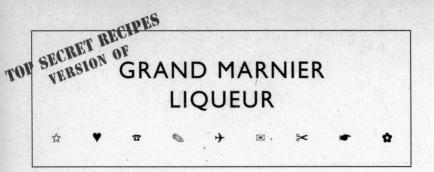

GRAND MARNIER LIQUEUR

☆ ♥ ☎ ✎ ✈ ✉ ✂ ☛ ✿

In 1880s France, oranges were quite rare and exotic. So when Louis Alexandre Marnier-Lopostolle traveled to the Caribbean in search of ingredients, he came back with bitter oranges to combine with his family's fine cognac. While other orange-flavored liqueurs such as triple sec and curaçao are mixed with a neutral alcohol base, Grand Marnier took it to the next level with a more complex flavor that makes it today's top-selling French liqueur.

Now you too can combine cognac with real orange to make a home version of this tasty (and pricey) stuff. By using an inexpensive cognac that costs around 18 to 20 dollars a bottle, you can create a clone cousin of the real thing that normally sells for 28 to 32 dollars a bottle. All you need, in addition to the cognac, is some sugar, an orange, and a little patience.

2 cups cognac   ⅔ cup granulated sugar
1 medium orange

1. Pour the cognac into a 2-cup jar with a lid.
2. Peel and section the orange, then slice each of the orange sections in half lengthwise, and add them to the jar along with the sugar.
3. Cover jar and shake until the sugar is dissolved.
4. Store the jar at room temperature for at least 2 weeks, then strain the orange slices and pulp from the liquid. Use as you would the real thing, for sipping or in mixed drinks.

• MAKES 2 CUPS.

HIRAM WALKER ANISETTE LIQUEUR

☆ ♥ ☎ ✎ ✈ ✉ ✄ ☞ ✿

For centuries anise has been a key ingredient in distilled spirits, and it is the most widely used flavor for drinks in countries surrounding the Mediterranean. Today it's used as the key flavoring ingredient in ouzo, sambuca, raki, Pernod, and a host of other international aperitifs and liqueurs. The availability of anise extract (found near the vanilla in most supermarkets) makes home cloning this popular brand of anisette liqueur an easy project.

½ cup very hot water
⅔ cup granulated sugar

1 cup 80-proof vodka
¼ teaspoon anise extract

1. Dissolve sugar in the hot water.
2. Add vodka and anise extract. Store in sealed container.

• MAKES 2 CUPS.

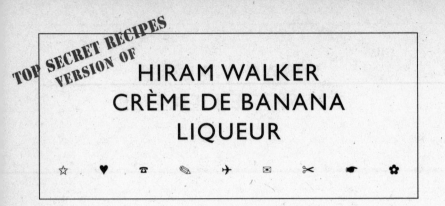

HIRAM WALKER CRÈME DE BANANA LIQUEUR

In the Cocktails section you'll find many recipes that require banana-flavored liqueur, a very common ingredient at the bars these days. Here's how to make some from scratch for your top secret concoctions if you don't feel like fetching the real thing.

¾ cup very hot water
¾ cup granulated sugar
1 cup 80-proof vodka

¼ teaspoon imitation banana
   extract
1 drop yellow food coloring

1. Combine the hot water with the sugar in a small pitcher. Stir until sugar is dissolved.
2. Add vodka, banana extract, and food coloring and stir well. Cool to room temperature before using. Store in a sealed container.

• MAKES 2 CUPS.

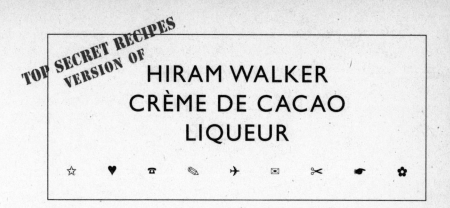

HIRAM WALKER CRÈME DE CACAO LIQUEUR

The chocolate taste in this liqueur comes from cocoa most commonly used for baking. After storing this liqueur for a week or so, we'll strain it through a coffee filter or a wire strainer that's been lined with paper towels to remove most of the cocoa. Sediment is not cool in liqueurs. Our finished product won't be quite as clear as the real thing, but the taste should be right there.

¾ cup very hot water
¾ cup plus 1 tablespoon
   granulated sugar

1 cup 80-proof vodka
2 tablespoons cocoa
½ teaspoon vanilla extract

1. Dissolve the sugar in the hot water.
2. Add the vodka, cocoa, and vanilla. Stir well. Store in a covered container for at least a week. Shake the liqueur every day or two.
3. Strain the liqueur through a coffee filter or paper towel–lined strainer into a bowl or pitcher. Store in a covered container.

• MAKES 2 CUPS.

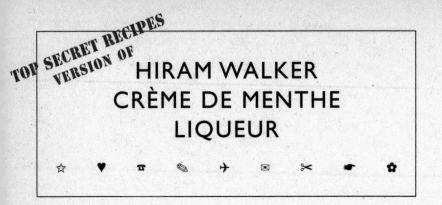

HIRAM WALKER CRÈME DE MENTHE LIQUEUR

☆   ♥   ☎   ✎   ✈   ✉   ✂   ☛   ✿

The popular mint liqueur is quick to make at home, and we'll even make it a deep, dark green like the real thing with 45 drops (or ½ teaspoon) of green food coloring. As for the mint flavoring, be sure to get "peppermint" extract, not "mint" extract.

½ cup very hot water
⅔ cup plus 1 tablespoon
   granulated sugar

1 cup 80-proof vodka
¾ teaspoon peppermint extract
45 drops green food coloring
   (½ teaspoon)

1. Dissolve the sugar in the hot water.
2. Add the vodka, peppermint extract, and food coloring. Store in a sealed container.

• MAKES 2 CUPS.

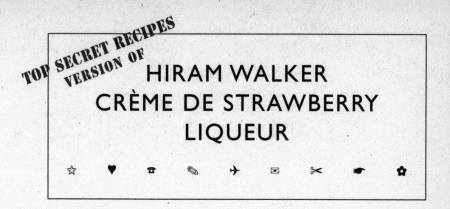

HIRAM WALKER CRÈME DE STRAWBERRY LIQUEUR

If you want to try a couple of good cocktails that use this fruity liqueur, check out the clone recipe for T.G.I. Friday's Banana Split Blender Blaster on page 213, or for Bahama Breeze Verry Berry Good on page 135.

1 cup very hot water	¾ teaspoon imitation strawberry
⅔ cup granulated sugar	extract
1 cup 80-proof vodka	

1. Dissolve the sugar in the hot water.
2. Add the vodka and strawberry extract. Stir well and store in a sealed container.

• MAKES 2½ CUPS.

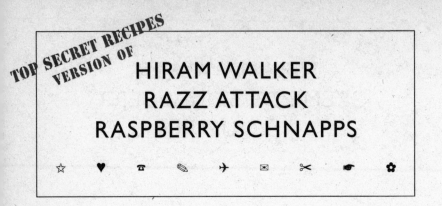

HIRAM WALKER
RAZZ ATTACK
RASPBERRY SCHNAPPS

☆　♥　☎　🖊　✈　🖂　✂　☛　✿

To make this delicious raspberry schnapps you'll need to track down the raspberry flavoring syrup used in coffeehouses with the brand name Torani. A few of the more popular flavors, raspberry included, are now available in most supermarkets.

1 cup very hot water	*½ cup Torani raspberry flavoring*
⅓ cup sugar	*syrup*
1 cup 80-proof vodka	

1. Dissolve the sugar in the hot water.
2. Add vodka and flavoring syrup and stir well. Store in a covered container.

• MAKES 2⅔ CUPS.

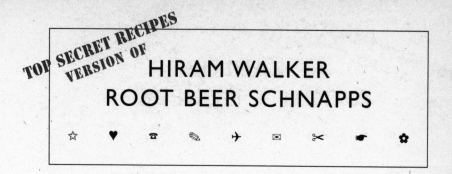

HIRAM WALKER
ROOT BEER SCHNAPPS

You could use this liqueur to make a teddy bear shooter: Layer ½ ounce of vodka over ½ ounce of root beer schnapps in a shot glass. Or you could make a root beer float as described on the bottle of the real Hiram Walker Root Beer Schnapps by adding 1 part Root Beer Schnapps to 2 parts milk or cream, and 4 parts 7UP or Sprite, then combining it all in a blender with ice until smooth. Or you could just pour it over some ice cream and dive in.

1 cup very hot water
¾ cup granulated sugar

1 cup 80-proof vodka
¼ teaspoon root beer concentrate

1. Dissolve the sugar in the hot water.
2. Add the vodka and root beer concentrate. Store in a sealed container.

• MAKES 2½ CUPS.

KAHLÚA
COFFEE LIQUEUR

☆ ♥ ☎ ✎ ✈ ✉ ✂ ☞ ✿

Kahlúa may market itself as the coffee liqueur developed in Mexico, but many believe the brand originated in Turkey. Looking at the label, we can still see an Arabic archway under which a sombrero-wearing man rests. Old labels of the brand show this man wearing a turban and smoking a pipe. Even the name *Kahlúa* is of Arabic origin. Regardless of where the drink came from, it dominates all other coffee liqueurs out there, including the very popular Tia Maria.

Here's a greatly improved version of the clone recipe that appears in *Top Secret Recipes*. You'll find this recipe is easier to make, tastes better, and, just as with the first recipe, improves with age.

1 cup light corn syrup	½ cup hot water
½ cup granulated sugar	1⅓ cups vodka
5 teaspoons instant coffee	1½ teaspoons vanilla extract

1. Combine corn syrup, sugar, and instant coffee with hot water in a medium pitcher or large jar. Stir or shake until sugar has dissolved.
2. Add vodka and vanilla extract and stir well. Store in a covered container.

• MAKES 3 CUPS.

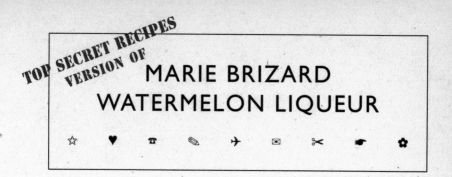

MARIE BRIZARD
WATERMELON LIQUEUR

This delicious brand of watermelon liqueur is easy to duplicate by pureeing fresh watermelon. You'll need a cup of pureed melon that comes from about ⅛ of a medium watermelon. I suggest you get the seedless kind.

1 cup pureed watermelon (no seeds)

½ cup plus 1 tablespoon granulated sugar

1 cup 80-proof vodka

1. Make pureed watermelon by removing the seeds and rind from about ⅛ of a medium watermelon (seedless watermelon is the easiest to use). Use a large fork or potato masher to mash the watermelon in a large bowl. You don't need to puree it in the bowl, just mash it up enough to create some liquid so that the fruit will puree well in the blender. Pour the melon and sugar into your blender and blend for 15 seconds or so, or until the sugar has dissolved.
2. Pour the watermelon puree into a container with a lid, add the vodka, and cover. Store at room temperature for a week.
3. Strain the melon pulp from the liquid by pouring it through a paper towel–lined strainer. Store in a sealed container.

• MAKES 2½ CUPS.

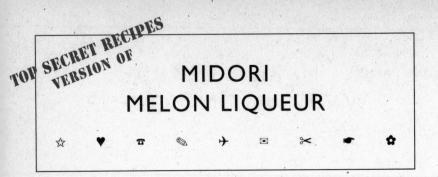

MIDORI
MELON LIQUEUR

☆ ♥ ☎ ✎ ✈ ✉ ✄ ☛ ✿

The world's most famous melon liqueur can be imitated at home by pureeing fresh honeydew melon. After the liqueur sits for a week or so, strain out the melon, put on your drinking cap, and enjoy thoroughly.

1 cup pureed honeydew melon	4 drops green food coloring
¾ cup granulated sugar	3 drops yellow food coloring
1 cup 80-proof vodka	

1. Puree the honeydew melon by first slicing ¼ of the melon away from the rind. Remove the seeds and then slice the melon into big chunks. Put the chunks into a medium bowl and mash with a potato masher to create some juice. Pour the mashed melon and juice into a blender and blend on medium speed for 10 to 15 seconds or until pureed. Measure 1 cup of melon into a jar with a lid.
2. Add sugar, vodka, and food coloring to the jar. Cover and shake until sugar is dissolved.
3. Store liqueur at room temperature for a week, then strain the melon pulp from the liquid by pouring it through a paper towel–lined strainer.

- MAKES 2 CUPS.

SPIRITS:
COCKTAILS

I'm fascinated by Prohibition. There's something intriguing about the way drinking alcoholic beverages in the United States reached a new level of hip when the federal government took away the right in 1920. Forever chiseled into history will be clear proof that when people are told too often how to live their lives, it has the reverse effect. Sure, you can take the cocaine out of their Coca-Cola, but stay the heck away from their whiskey.

Before Prohibition drinking was mostly a man's sport. The drinks were pretty dull, and they were usually made with whiskey. When the cocktail parties went underground as fancy private shindigs and secret speakeasies, women got into the party full swing, and many of the mixed drinks that are still around today were invented at those gatherings using creative new ingredients.

At that time, gangs ran the liquor industry. Bootleggers imported alcohol into the country and got filthy rich. Murders, beatings, and bribery were commonplace. Shipments of booze were smuggled secretly into the U.S. from Canada and the Caribbean, and homemade distilleries were built in darkened cellars and on backwoods riverbanks. Many local governments and law enforcement officials got on the gangs' payroll and looked the other way. Some joined in on the party because even they thought the law was lame.

The United States lost somewhere around 500 million dollars in whiskey taxes every year during Prohibition and the economy skidded into a deep depression. When the government realized that Prohibition was causing more harm than good, the

Eighteenth Amendment was repealed by the Twenty-first in 1933, and the bars reopened for business. By then, though, the damage was done.

Since American distilleries had shut down, European booze-makers captured the U.S. market by immediately flooding the country with their own brands. Some domestic distillers struggled to start from scratch again, only to be forced to shut down during World War II to produce industrial alcohol for the war effort.

After the war, the distilling industry finally got back on its feet. A wider variety of spirits were in demand and the market's taste shifted from the old standards of whiskey, rum, and gin. Vodka became the number one spirit in the later decades of the twentieth century as a new generation of drinkers enjoyed festive happy hours with fancy designer libations that edged out old cocktail formulations their parents used to drink.

Newsweek and *The Saturday Evening Post* reported that the beginning of the "singles age" started when the first T.G.I. Friday's opened in New York City in 1965. Bars in growing casual restaurant chains became hot spots every night of the week where the professional crowd gathered after a hard day's work.

The ability to quickly serve up a well-mixed cocktail with flair from an expanding number of combinations had grown into a welcomed and appreciated social art form, even overcoming a slight setback in 1988 as the subject of a really bad Tom Cruise flick.

HOW TO USE THIS SECTION

In this section I'll show you how to use your home bar to re-create the most popular drinks from the country's biggest and fastest-growing casual restaurant chains. For years now companies have been bottling mixers to make home bartending a simpler task. But you should know that many of the restaurant chains make their own mixers from scratch at the beginning of each business day. So to create the tastiest cocktails at home, you should take the extra time to make all your mixers—sweet & sour, pina colada mix, and mai tai mix—using the simple recipes in the last section of the book. It's definitely worth the extra effort, especially if you're hosting a little bash.

You'll also need some jiggers if you want to mix good drinks from this book. As with any proper cocktail guide, I've listed the ingredients in ounces. A two-sided metal jigger is easy to find at liquor stores and supermarkets, and it's cheap. First find one with 1 ounce on one side and 1½ ounces on the other side. Then you might also get one with ¾ ounce and 1¼-ounce measurements.

In case you don't have a jigger and want to get on with the mixing, never fear. I've got a chart here that converts ounces so that you can mix your drinks using tablespoons and cups. Also, I've conveniently included cup equivalents in the recipes (in parentheses) for all measurements of 2 ounces or more.

> ½ ounce = 1 tablespoon
> ¾ ounce = 1½ tablespoons
> 1 ounce = 2 tablespoons
> 1¼ ounces = 2½ tablespoons
> 1½ ounces = 3 tablespoons
> 2 ounces = ¼ cup
> 3 ounces = approx. ⅓ cup
> 4 ounces = ½ cup
> 6 ounces = ¾ cup
> 8 ounces = 1 cup

You'll notice that brand names for spirits and sodas are specified in many of the recipes. Usually it's because the restaurant has marketed the drink with those particular ingredients. For an exact clone, you should use the same brands. But, as a general rule, your drinks won't suffer if you replace the Smirnoff vodka, for example, with whatever vodka you've got in the bar. As well, you can use any cola where Coke is specified (such as Pepsi), and any lemon-lime soda where 7UP is listed (such as Sprite), and vice-versa. But try to use Kern's nectars for recipes that require it, and when you shop for cranberry juice cocktail, always go with Ocean Spray.

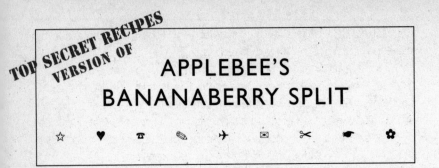

APPLEBEE'S BANANABERRY SPLIT

The secret to re-creating many of Applebee's drinks is to stay away from the bottled cocktail mixers and make your own from scratch. The recipe for the pina colada mix is a simple 2-to-1 ratio of pineapple juice to cream of coconut and can be found on page 230. You'll be making two drinks here, so have a companion ready.

2 ripe bananas
1 10-ounce box frozen sweetened
   sliced strawberries, thawed
3 ounces Captain Morgan spiced
   rum
2 cups ice

⅓ cup pina colada mix (from
   page 230)

GARNISH
2 fresh whole strawberries
whipped cream

1. Cut an end off each banana—set these smaller pieces aside to use as a garnish later—then put the rest of the bananas into a blender.
2. Add the remaining ingredients to the blender and blend until the ice is crushed and the drink is smooth.
3. Pour the drinks into two stemmed drink glasses—such as daiquiri glasses—and add a banana piece and fresh strawberry to the rim of each glass. Add a dollop of whipped cream on top of each drink and serve with a straw.

• MAKES 2 DRINKS.

APPLEBEE'S BLUE SKIES

Check this out. The blue curaçao is drizzled over the top of the white frozen pina colada–like drink, then it slides down the inside of the glass with groovy lava lamp flair.

1 cup ice
6 ounces (¾ cup) pina colada
   mix (from page 230)
1½ ounces peach schnapps
½ ounce blue curaçao liqueur

GARNISH
1 pineapple slice
1 pineapple leaf

1. Combine one cup of ice with pina colada mix and peach schnapps in a blender. Blend on high speed until ice is crushed and the drink is smooth.
2. Pour the drink into a white wine glass.
3. Invert the bowl of a spoon just over the rim of the drink. Carefully pour ½ ounce of blue curaçao over the back of the spoon so that it rests on top of the drink. The blue stuff will slowly fall down around the edge of the drink. You can trip out on this for a while, but don't go too long since we still need to garnish.
4. Slice halfway into a fresh pineapple slice and display it on the rim of the glass. Add a pineapple leaf into the top of the drink, if you've got it, then add a straw and serve.

• MAKES 1 DRINK.

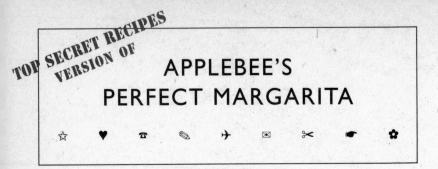

APPLEBEE'S
PERFECT MARGARITA

You'll need a cocktail shaker for this one. And if you want to serve it up the same way as in the restaurant you also need a small martini glass. This recipe involves making sweet & sour mix from scratch with fresh lemons and limes following the recipe on page 231. You'll also need some simple syrup to sweeten the drink. That's a basic common recipe requiring two parts sugar to one part boiling water. You'll have some leftover ingredients for an additional serving if you like. And once you taste this, you'll like.

1 cup ice
1¼ ounces Cuervo 1800 Añejo
   tequila
¾ ounce Cointreau liqueur
¾ ounce Grand Marnier liqueur
1 ounce fresh lime juice
1 ounce simple syrup (from
   page 226)

6 ounces (¾ cup) sweet & sour
   mix (from page 231)

GARNISH
margarita salt
lime wedge
olive

1. Put ice in a shaker, followed by the tequila, Cointreau, Grand Marnier, and 1 ounce of fresh lime juice. Add 1 ounce of simple syrup and 6 ounces (¾ cup) of sweet & sour mix to the shaker. Shake well.
2. Salt the rim of a martini glass if you'd like. Spear a lime wedge and olive with a toothpick and drop it in the glass. Pour the drink into the glass through a strainer, and serve the cocktail with the rest of the drink in the shaker on the side.

• SERVES 1.

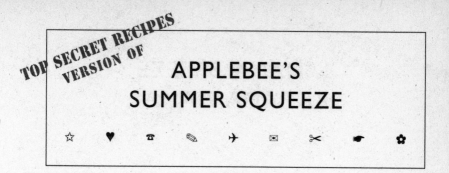

APPLEBEE'S
SUMMER SQUEEZE

☆ ♥ ☎ ✎ ✈ ✉ ✄ ☛ ✿

For this drink, make the lemonade from scratch to re-create that familiar Applebee's barstool experience. Okay, so maybe it's just familiar to me, and I probably shouldn't go around announcing it. This recipe makes two drinks.

LEMONADE
4 ounces (½ cup) fresh lemon juice (from 2 to 3 lemons)
¼ cup granulated sugar
2 cups water

3 ounces Bacardi Limon rum
6 lemon wedges

1. Prepare lemonade by combining the fresh lemon juice, sugar, and water in a small pitcher. Stir until sugar dissolves.
2. Make drinks by filling each of two 16-ounce glasses with ice. Add 1½ ounces of Bacardi Limon to each glass and fill to the top with lemonade. Squeeze two lemon wedges into each glass, and then drop the wedges into the drink. Put a slice in each of the remaining two lemon wedges and add one to the rim of each glass. Serve 'em up with straws and a smile.

• MAKES 2 DRINKS.

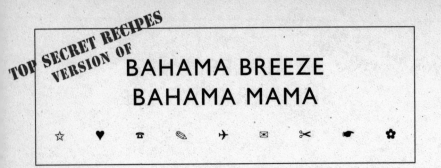

BAHAMA BREEZE
BAHAMA MAMA

Be sure to use freshly squeezed orange juice if you want this to be a true cocktail replica. Bahama Breeze bartenders not only squeeze fresh orange juice for these famous drinks, but they also operate a sugar cane juice extractor to produce sweet nectar for other tasty libations and non-alcoholic sips.

½ ounce Malibu rum
½ ounce Myers's dark rum
½ ounce Bacardi light rum
½ ounce banana liqueur
2 ounces (¼ cup) pineapple juice

2 ounces (¼ cup) freshly
  squeezed orange juice (about
  ½ of a large orange)
splash Sprite

GARNISH
pineapple slice

1. Fill a 14-ounce glass with ice.
2. Pour all ingredients, except Sprite, into a shaker. Shake well and pour over ice.
3. Add a splash of Sprite on top. Garnish with a pineapple slice on the rim of the glass, add a straw, and serve.

• MAKES 1 DRINK.

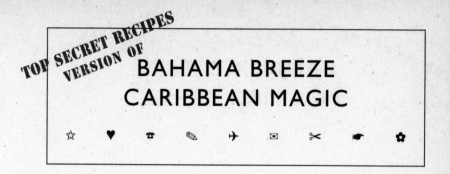

BAHAMA BREEZE
CARIBBEAN MAGIC

Prepare to clone another Bahama Breeze favorite. Use fresh orange juice to properly re-create the magic.

1 ounce vodka
½ ounce amaretto liqueur
½ ounce Southern Comfort
1½ ounces sweet & sour mix
  (from page 231)
1½ ounces pineapple juice

2 ounces (¼ cup) freshly
  squeezed orange juice
splash cranberry juice

GARNISH
pineapple slice

1. Fill a 14-ounce glass with ice.
2. Combine all ingredients, except cranberry juice, in a shaker and shake well. Pour over ice.
3. Add a splash of cranberry juice, garnish with a pineapple slice, and serve with a straw.

• MAKES 1 DRINK.

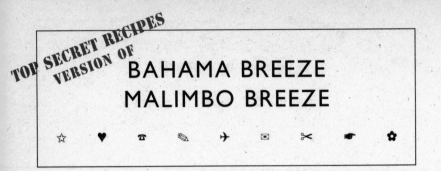

BAHAMA BREEZE
MALIMBO BREEZE

☆ ♥ ☎ ✎ ✈ ✉ ✂ ☛ ✿

A tropical wind of flavors blows over your tongue and soothes like a cool island ... ah, just drink it.

1 ¼ ounces Malibu rum
¾ ounce triple sec liqueur
2 ounces (¼ cup) pineapple juice
2 ounces (¼ cup) freshly
  squeezed orange juice

splash Rose's lime juice
splash cranberry juice

GARNISH
pineapple slice

1. Fill a 14-ounce glass with ice.
2. Combine all ingredients, except lime juice and cranberry juice, in a shaker and shake well. Pour over ice.
3. Add a splash of Rose's lime juice and cranberry juice, garnish with a pineapple slice on the rim, and serve with a straw.

• MAKES 1 DRINK.

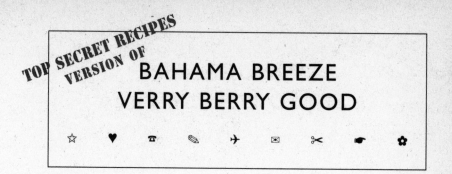

BAHAMA BREEZE
VERRY BERRY GOOD

A delicious frozen berry drink that'll make you a verry bad speller.

1 ounce strawberry schnapps
½ ounce DeKuyper Razzmatazz
  schnapps
½ ounce blueberry schnapps
⅓ cup frozen raspberries

3 ounces sweet & sour mix (from
  page 228)
½ cup ice

GARNISH
pineapple slice

1. Combine all ingredients in a blender. Blend until ice is crushed and drink is smooth.
2. Pour into a 12-ounce glass, and garnish with a pineapple slice on the rim. Serve with a straw.

• MAKES 1 DRINK.

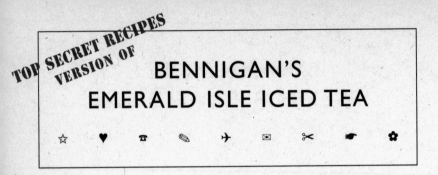

BENNIGAN'S EMERALD ISLE ICED TEA

☆　♥　☎　✎　✈　✉　✂　☜　✿

Here's a great version of Long Island Iced Tea with an Irish twist that's loved by all twisted Irish.

½ ounce Cointreau liqueur
½ ounce Skyy vodka
½ ounce Captain Morgan spiced rum
½ ounce Jameson Irish whiskey

4 ounces (½ cup) sweet & sour mix (from page 231)
1 ounce Coca-Cola

GARNISH
lemon wedge

1. Fill a 14-ounce glass with ice. Add all ingredients in the order listed.
2. Garnish with a lemon wedge and serve with a straw.

• MAKES 1 DRINK.

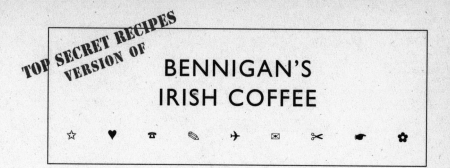

BENNIGAN'S IRISH COFFEE

☆　♥　☎　✎　✈　✉　✂　☛　✿

Time for the ultimate Irish coffee clone recipe from the country's favorite Irish-themed chain restaurant. It wakes you up, takes you down, kicks you around, and looks great with green crème de menthe drizzled over the whipped cream and a nice little cherry hat.

1 ounce Jameson Irish whiskey
½ ounce Kahlúa liqueur
10 ounces hot coffee
whipped cream

splash crème de menthe

GARNISH
maraschino cherry

1. Pour the whiskey and Kahlúa into a coffee cup.
2. Add coffee to the top of the cup.
3. Squirt a big pile of whipped cream on top of the coffee.
4. Drizzle crème de menthe over the whipped cream.
5. Garnish with a cherry on top of the whipped cream and serve.

• MAKES 1 DRINK.

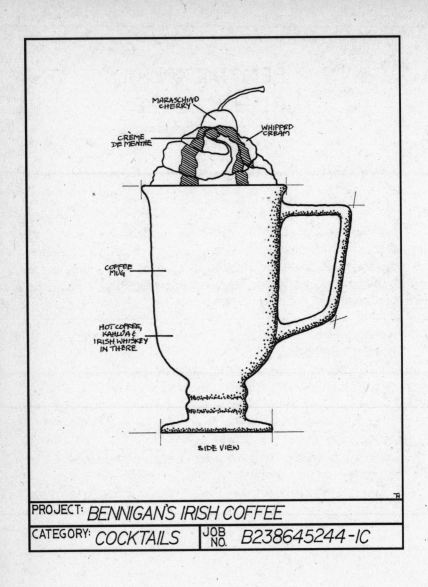

MARASCHINO CHERRY

WHIPPED CREAM

CRÈME DE MENTHE

COFFEE MUG

HOT COFFEE, KAHLÚA & IRISH WHISKEY IN THERE

SIDE VIEW

PROJECT:	*BENNIGAN'S IRISH COFFEE*		
CATEGORY: *COCKTAILS*	JOB NO.	*B238645244-IC*	

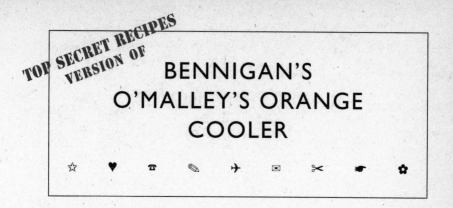

BENNIGAN'S O'MALLEY'S ORANGE COOLER

This drink is an overdue improvement on the old-school screw-driver. Mix this with orange-flavored vodka, add a little sugar and Sprite, and you've got a tastier new twist on a tired old favorite.

1 ½ ounces Absolut Mandrin
   vodka
4 ounces (½ cup) orange juice
1 packet (1 teaspoon) sugar or
   sweetener
1 ounce Sprite

GARNISH
orange wedge
maraschino cherry

1. Fill a 14-ounce glass with ice.
2. Combine the vodka, orange juice, and sugar in a shaker. Shake well and pour over ice.
3. Add Sprite on top of drink, garnish with an orange wedge and maraschino cherry speared on a toothpick. Serve with a straw.

• MAKES 1 DRINK.

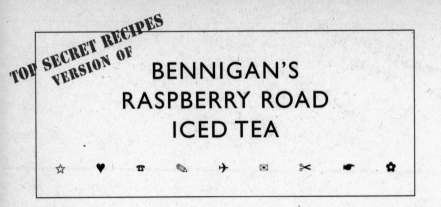

BENNIGAN'S
RASPBERRY ROAD
ICED TEA

☆　♥　☎　✎　✈　✉　✂　☛　✿

Bennigan's tweaks the Long Island Iced Tea with this Chambord-laced beauty.

½ ounce Skyy vodka
½ ounce Beefeater gin
½ ounce triple sec liqueur
½ ounce Chambord raspberry
   liqueur

4 ounces (½ cup) sweet & sour
   mix (from page 231)
1 ounce Coca-Cola

GARNISH
1 lemon wedge

1. Fill a 14-ounce glass with ice.
2. Pour all ingredients over ice in the order listed.
3. Garnish with a lemon wedge and serve with a straw.

• MAKES 1 DRINK.

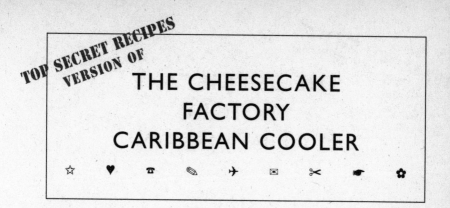

THE CHEESECAKE FACTORY CARIBBEAN COOLER

☆ ♥ ☎ ✎ ✈ ✉ ✂ ☛ ✿

This recipe clones a delicious smoothie-type cocktail using strawberry puree that you make from a thawed box of the frozen sliced strawberries. One ounce of puree goes into the glass first before you add the drink. Check out the cool layering effect.

1 cup ice
¾ ounce white rum
¾ ounce Malibu rum
1¼ ounces cream of coconut
1¼ ounces half-and-half
2 ounces (¼ cup) mango juice
2 ounces (¼ cup) pineapple juice

2 ounces (¼ cup) strawberry
  puree

GARNISH
whole strawberry
orange slice
pineapple slice

1. Make the strawberry puree by thawing frozen sweetened sliced strawberries. Blend until smooth.
2. Combine ice, rums, coconut, half-and-half, mango juice, pineapple juice, and half (1 ounce) of the strawberry puree in a blender and blend on high speed until the ice is crushed and the drink is smooth.
3. Pour the remaining 1 ounce of strawberry puree into the bottom of a 14-ounce wine glass.
4. Pour the drink into the glass over the strawberry puree. Add the strawberry, orange slice, and pineapple slice to the rim of the glass. Add a straw and serve.

• MAKES 1 DRINK.

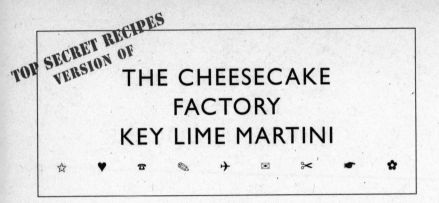

THE CHEESECAKE FACTORY KEY LIME MARTINI

It's like eating a key lime pie, except there's no crust, it looks like a martini, and you're drinking it. For the whipped cream in this recipe be sure to use the canned kind with a nozzle top. Estimate about a cup's worth into the shaker with everything else and shake it up real good.

1½ ounces Vox vodka
½ ounce Midori liqueur
½ ounce white crème de cacao
   liqueur
juice of ½ lime
1 ounce simple syrup (from
   page 226)

1 cup canned whipped cream
   (nozzle top)

GARNISH
sugar for rim
whole lime slice

1. Chill a martini glass by filling it with ice and water.
2. Add all the ingredients into a shaker, along with a handful of ice, and shake well.
3. Remove ice and water from the martini glass, then moisten just half of the rim of the glass and dip it into sugar.
4. Strain drink into the glass, and add a lime slice to the sugared side of the rim (so that the drink is sipped from the unsugared edge), and serve.

• MAKES 1 DRINK.

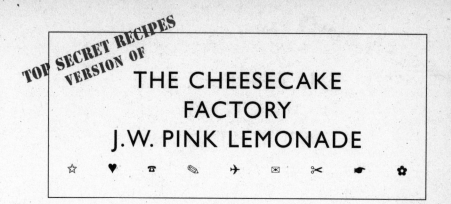

THE CHEESECAKE FACTORY
J.W. PINK LEMONADE

☆ ♥ ☎ ✎ ✈ ✉ ✂ ☞ ✿

This drink is named after the bartender who invented it over nine years ago: Mr. Jeff Wiley, of the Redondo Beach, California, Cheesecake Factory. He's still there inventing killer drinks, but none have been as successful as this cocktail, which is currently one of the top five best-selling drinks at the chain.

If you don't want to make lemonade from scratch and want something that tastes similar to the stuff used at the Factory, pick up Country Time lemonade. If you've got time to take the fresh-squeezed route, check out the fresh lemonade recipes on pages 88–90.

1 ½ ounces Absolut Citron vodka
½ ounce Chambord liqueur
6 ounces (¾ cup) Country Time
   lemonade

GARNISH
sugar for rim
lemon wedge

1. Moisten the rim of a 16-ounce glass. Dip the rim in sugar then fill it with ice.
2. Add the ingredients in the order listed, garnish with a lemon wedge, and serve with a straw.

• MAKES 1 DRINK.

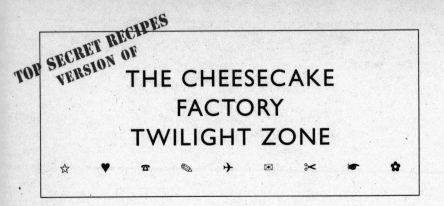

THE CHEESECAKE FACTORY TWILIGHT ZONE

☆ ♥ ☎ ◇ ✈ ✉ ✂ ☞ ✿

Next stop ... this crazy drink. Looking at this list of ingredients, you just know it's going to end with an ironic, thought-provoking twist.

½ ounce Bacardi light rum
½ ounce Myers's dark rum
½ ounce crème de cacao liqueur
¼ ounce Bacardi 151 rum
¼ ounce triple sec liqueur
¼ ounce amaretto liqueur
2 ounces (¼ cup) mango juice
2 ounces (¼ cup) orange juice

2 ounces (¼ cup) pineapple juice
splash grenadine

GARNISH
lime wedge
orange slice
maraschino cherry

1. Fill a 16-ounce glass with ice.
2. Add all the ingredients in the order listed.
3. Drop in lime wedge, orange slice, and maraschino cherry. Serve with a straw.

• MAKES 1 DRINK.

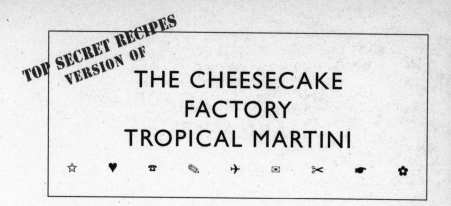

THE CHEESECAKE FACTORY TROPICAL MARTINI

☆ ♥ ☎ ✎ ✈ ✉ ✂ ☞ ✿

This drink weaves together the sophistication of a martini with the loose fruity fun of a tasty tropical number. If you can't find straight passion fruit juice, pick up a passion fruit blend, such as Mauna Lai Paradise Passion guava/passion fruit blend, and make one of these immediately.

2 ounces vodka
2 ounces passion fruit juice
1 ounce mango juice
1 ounce pineapple juice
½ ounce simple syrup (from page 226)

splash grenadine

GARNISH
sugar for rim
whole strawberry
pineapple slice

1. Chill a martini glass by filling it with ice and water.
2. Add all the ingredients into a shaker, along with some ice, and shake well.
3. Remove ice and water from martini glass, then moisten half of the rim of the glass and dip it into sugar.
4. Strain drink into the glass, add a strawberry and pineapple slice to the sugared side of the rim (so that the drink is sipped from the unsugared edge), and serve.

• MAKES 1 DRINK.

CHEVYS
100% BLUE AGAVE
MARGARITA

If you want to enjoy a really good margarita get to a Mexican food chain and order it "on the rocks." The rocks versions are usually made with top shelf tequilas, rather than the cheaper stuff found in the slushy blended kind. Create your next margarita masterpiece with this bright blue dazzler, or with one of the other happy Chevys clone recipes that follow.

1 ½ ounces Herradura silver
   tequila
½ ounce triple sec liqueur
½ ounce blue curaçao liqueur
½ cup sweet & sour mix (from
   page 231)

OPTIONAL
salt around the rim

GARNISH
lime wedge

1. Put a handful of ice into a shaker.
2. Add all ingredients and shake. Pour the drink into a 12-ounce margarita glass (salt the rim first, if you want it).
3. Garnish with a lime wedge on a toothpick, add a straw, and serve.

- MAKES 1 DRINK.

CHEVYS
HOUSE ROCKS
MARGARITA

☆　♥　☎　✎　✈　✉　✂　☛　✿

This formula re-creates the chain's basic rocks margarita. Nothing fancy, but still good when you use freshly made sweet & sour.

1 ½ ounces El Jimador silver
   tequila
½ ounce triple sec liqueur
½ cup sweet & sour mix (from
   page 231)

OPTIONAL
salt around the rim

GARNISH
lime wedge

1. Put a handful of ice into a shaker.
2. Add all ingredients and shake. Pour the drink into a 12-ounce margarita glass (salt the rim first, if you want it).
3. Garnish with a lime wedge on a toothpick, add a straw, and serve.

• Makes 1 drink.

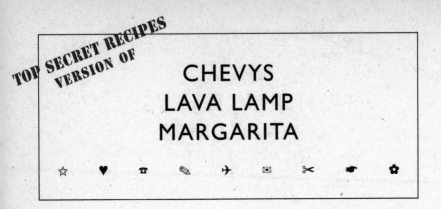

CHEVYS
LAVA LAMP
MARGARITA

This one gets its name from the look of the Chambord that's added to the glass after the drink is mixed. Drizzled on top of the drink, the tasty raspberry liqueur serpentines in slow-mo to the bottom of the glass. Since the drink is served layered, instruct your designated drinker to stir before sipping, or get a mouthful of lava.

1½ ounces Sauza
   Conmemorativo tequila añejo
½ ounce triple sec liqueur
½ cup sweet & sour mix (from
   page 231)
½ ounce Chambord liqueur

OPTIONAL
salt around the rim

GARNISH
lime wedge

1. Put a handful of ice into a shaker.
2. Add tequila, triple sec, and sweet & sour mix to the shaker, shake, then pour the drink into a 12-ounce margarita glass (add salt around the rim of the glass first if you want it).
3. Drizzle Chambord into the glass, add a lime wedge on a toothpick, add a straw, and serve.

- MAKES 1 DRINK.

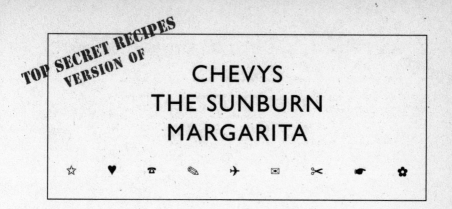

CHEVYS
THE SUNBURN
MARGARITA

Here's a sweeter margarita for tequila lovers with a cranberry fetish.

1 ½ ounces El Jimador silver
   tequila
½ ounce triple sec liqueur
¼ cup sweet & sour mix (from
   page 231)
¼ cup cranberry juice

OPTIONAL
salt around the rim

GARNISH
lime wedge

1. Put a handful of ice into a shaker.
2. Add all ingredients, shake, and pour the drink into a 12-ounce margarita glass (salt the rim first, if you want it).
3. Garnish with a lime wedge on a toothpick, add a straw, and serve.

• MAKES 1 DRINK.

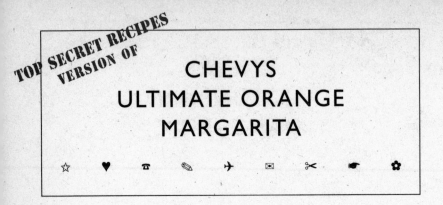

CHEVYS
ULTIMATE ORANGE
MARGARITA

If by delicious you mean Herradura tequila, Cointreau, orange juice, and homemade sweet & sour mix, then, yes, this margarita is quite delicious.

1½ ounces Herradura reposado
  tequila
½ ounce Cointreau liqueur
2 ounces (¼ cup) orange juice
2 ounces (¼ cup) sweet & sour
  mix (from page 231)

OPTIONAL
salt around the rim

GARNISH
lime wedge

1. Put a handful of ice into a shaker.
2. Add all ingredients and shake. Pour the drink into a 12-ounce margarita glass (salt the rim first, if you want it).
3. Garnish with a lime wedge on a toothpick, add a straw, and serve.

- MAKES 1 DRINK.

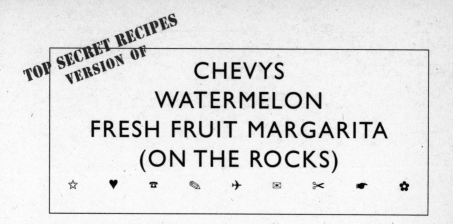

CHEVYS WATERMELON FRESH FRUIT MARGARITA (ON THE ROCKS)

☆　♥　☎　✎　✈　⊠　✂　☛　✿

Chevys is famous for margaritas made with fresh, pureed fruits. While these drinks usually come in blended form combined with house margarita mix right out of a machine, they are much better when ordered on the rocks. Here now is a clone of the most popular flavor, watermelon, made by simply pureeing some fresh melon in your blender. First cut some ripe seedless watermelon from the rind, and then coarsely smash it in a bowl with a potato masher or large fork (this gives the blender something to grab on to). Pour the melon from the bowl into a blender and blend on high speed for 10 seconds or until the watermelon is pureed.

1 ½ ounces El Jimador silver
　tequila
½ ounce triple sec liqueur
2 ounces (¼ cup) sweet & sour
　mix (from page 231)

2 ounces (½ cup) pureed
　watermelon (seedless)

GARNISH
lime wedge

1. Put a handful of ice into a shaker.
2. Add all ingredients and shake. Pour the drink over ice in a 10-ounce margarita glass.
3. Garnish with a lime wedge on a toothpick and serve.

• MAKES 1 DRINK.

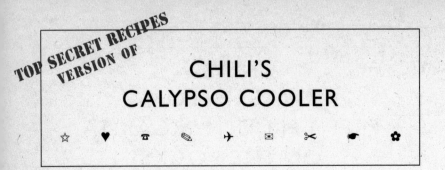

CHILI'S
CALYPSO COOLER

☆ ♥ ☎ ✎ ✈ ✉ ✂ ☞ ✿

Ever order one of those expensive specialty drinks off the shiny, full-color restaurant table-stand cards and wish you had a clone recipe? This is one of those drinks, off one of those cards. And here's the clone recipe.

1¼ ounces Captain Morgan
   spiced rum
½ ounce peach schnapps
4 ounces (½ cup) orange juice
splash Rose's lime juice

½ ounce grenadine

GARNISH
orange wedge
maraschino cherry

1. Fill a 16-ounce glass with ice.
2. Pour all ingredients over ice in order listed. Don't stir.
3. Garnish with an orange wedge and cherry on a toothpick. Serve with a straw.

• MAKES 1 DRINK.

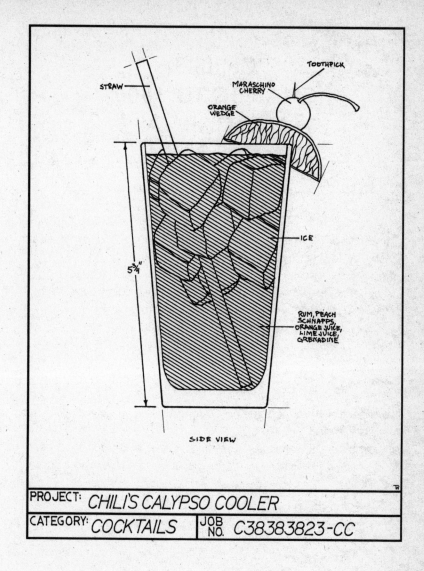

STRAW

TOOTHPICK

MARASCHINO
CHERRY

ORANGE
WEDGE

ICE

5¾"

RUM, PEACH
SCHNAPPS,
ORANGE JUICE,
LIME JUICE,
GRENADINE

SIDE VIEW

PROJECT: *CHILI'S CALYPSO COOLER*

CATEGORY: *COCKTAILS* **JOB NO.** *C38383823-CC*

CHILI'S CHAMBORD 1800 MARGARITA

☆   ♥   ☎   ✎   ✈   ✉   ✂   ☛   ✿

Meet the drink that comes in a giant 21-ounce "schooner" glass at Chili's. Now go find something big enough to hold it.

2½ ounces Cuervo 1800 Añejo
   tequila
¾ ounce Cointreau liqueur
1 ounce Chambord liqueur

4 ounces (½ cup) sweet & sour
   mix (from page 231)
splash Rose's lime juice

GARNISH
lime wedge

1. Prepare a 21-ounce glass by salting the rim if desired. Fill the glass with ice.
2. Combine all ingredients in a shaker, shake, and pour over ice.
3. Garnish with a lime wedge on the rim and serve with a straw.

• MAKES 1 21-OUNCE DRINK.

CHILI'S
JAMAICAN PARADISE

Thanks to Chili's you can catch a Jamaica-style buzz without leaving the States.

1 ¼ ounces Malibu rum
½ ounce Sauza gold tequila
½ ounce Midori liqueur
½ ounce blue curaçao liqueur
2 ounces (¼ cup) sweet & sour
   mix (from page 231)

splash Rose's lime juice

GARNISH
orange wedge
maraschino cherry

1. Fill a 16-ounce mug with ice.
2. Combine all ingredients in a shaker, shake, and pour over ice.
3. Add an orange wedge and maraschino cherry on a toothpick. Serve with a straw.

• MAKES 1 DRINK.

CHILI'S
MANDRIN BLUSH

☆ ♥ ☎ ✎ ✈ ✉ ✂ ☞ ✿

The subtle orange flavor combines well with the cranberry juice and Sprite. The vodka combines well with you.

1 ½ ounces Absolut Mandrin
   vodka
2 ounces (¼ cup) cranberry juice
4 ounces (½ cup) Sprite

GARNISH
orange wedge

1. Combine all ingredients in a shaker, shake, and pour into an ice-filled 16-ounce glass.
2. Garnish with an orange wedge on the rim and serve with a straw.

• MAKES 1 DRINK.

CHILI'S MARGARITA PRESIDENTE

☆ ♥ ☎ ✎ ✈ ✉ ✂ ☛ ✿

The Margarita Presidente is Chili's fancy designer libation made from Sauza Conmemorativo, Cointreau, and Presidente brandy. It's served up in a salt-rimmed martini glass along with additional servings in a shaker on the side. The drink comes highly recommended by the dozens of placards and signs dangling from rafters overhead in Chili's bar. I do concur.

This clone recipe should fill your glass around three times, and your head with many happy thoughts.

1 ¼ ounces Sauza
 Conmemorativo tequila añejo
½ ounce Cointreau liqueur
½ ounce Presidente brandy
4 ounces (½ cup) sweet & sour
 mix (from page 231)

splash Rose's lime juice

GARNISH
lime wedge

1. Combine all ingredients in a shaker with crushed ice. Shake.
2. Pour drink into an ice-filled martini glass rimmed with salt. Add a lime wedge and serve the remainder of the drink in the shaker on the side.

• SERVES 1.

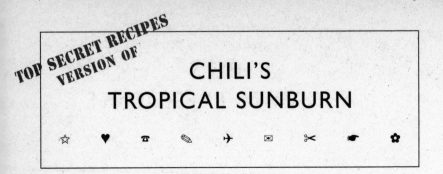

CHILI'S
TROPICAL SUNBURN

☆　♥　☎　✎　✈　✉　✂　☞　✿

The rums, Cointreau, and juices create an island flavor that anyone will love. This drink is named after its tendency to leave you passed out on the beach before applying sunscreen.

1¼ ounces Captain Morgan
　　spiced rum
¾ ounce Myers's dark rum
¾ ounce Cointreau liqueur
2 ounces (¼ cup) cranberry juice
2 ounces (¼ cup) pineapple juice

2 ounces (¼ cup) sweet & sour
　　mix (from page 231)

GARNISH
maraschino cherry

1. Combine all ingredients in a shaker, shake, and pour into an ice-filled 16-ounce glass or mug.
2. Garnish with a maraschino cherry, add a straw, and serve.

• MAKES 1 DRINK.

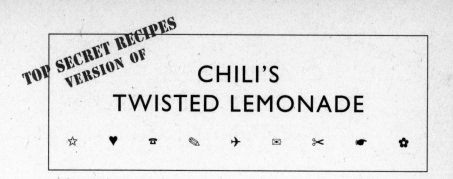

CHILI'S
TWISTED LEMONADE

Bars across the country are finding clever new ways to use the growing number of flavor-infused vodkas. Here's one simple, delicious example.

1 ¼ ounces Smirnoff Citrus Twist
  vodka
¾ ounce triple sec liqueur
3 ounces sweet & sour mix (from
  page 231)

GARNISH
lemon wedge

1. Fill a 14-ounce glass with crushed ice. Add vodka and triple sec.
2. Top off the drink with sweet & sour mix.
3. Add a lemon wedge garnish and serve with a straw.

• MAKES 1 DRINK.

TIDBITS

You can also add a splash of cranberry juice to make this a pink lemonade twist.

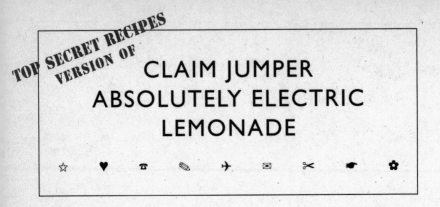

CLAIM JUMPER ABSOLUTELY ELECTRIC LEMONADE

Tastes like lemonade, buzzes like booze. Use one of the fresh lemonade clones from pages 88–90 for this one, or a pre-made lemonade when on time-sensitive missions.

2 ounces Absolut Citron vodka
1 ounce blue curaçao liqueur
6 ounces (¾ cup) fresh lemonade
  (from pages 88–90)

GARNISH
1 lemon slice

1. Fill a 16-ounce glass with ice.
2. Pour all ingredients in the order listed over the ice.
3. Garnish the rim with a lemon slice that has been slit with a knife to the middle. Add a straw and serve.

- MAKES 1 DRINK.

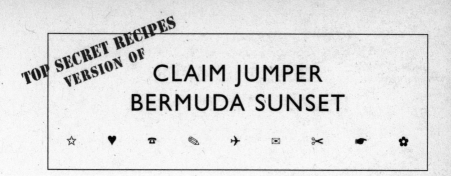

CLAIM JUMPER
BERMUDA SUNSET

Tropical drinks are everywhere, with nearly every chain restaurant offering at least a few variations. If you're a single guy, though, you might want to drink them at home. Tall, fruity drinks like this one taste great and hit hard, but it's tough to look cool sipping a towering pink cocktail sporting a paper umbrella fruit garnish.

½ ounce Absolut vodka
½ ounce Bacardi Limon rum
½ ounce Midori liqueur
½ ounce peach schnapps
2 ounces (¼ cup) pineapple juice
2 ounces (¼ cup) orange juice
2 ounces (¼ cup) cranberry juice

splash Bacardi 151 rum

GARNISH
pineapple slice
maraschino cherry
paper umbrella

1. Fill a 16-ounce glass with ice.
2. Pour all ingredients over ice in the order listed.
3. Add a garnish of pineapple slice and maraschino cherry on a paper umbrella. Serve with a straw.

• MAKES 1 DRINK.

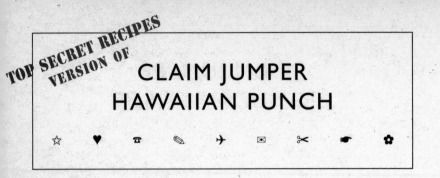

CLAIM JUMPER
HAWAIIAN PUNCH

It tastes just like Hawaiian Punch. Except this one can really punch.

½ ounce Southern Comfort
½ ounce sloe gin
½ ounce amaretto liqueur
3 ounces pineapple juice
3 ounces orange juice
splash Bacardi 151 Rum

GARNISH
pineapple juice
maraschino cherry
paper umbrella

1. Fill a 16-ounce glass with ice.
2. Pour all ingredients over ice in the order listed. Do not stir.
3. Garnish with a pineapple slice and maraschino cherry speared on a paper umbrella. Serve·with a straw.

• MAKES 1 DRINK.

CLAIM JUMPER
MAI TAI

This cocktail requires the homemade mai tai mix from page 229, which should tell you from the start that it's going to be good. Of course you can go the lazy route and use a pre-made mixer, like the one made by Mr & Mrs T. But I've got to say, there's nothing like the smooth, fruity taste that comes from the homemade fresh stuff. If you want to serve your guests a masterful mai tai, take the time to really make it rock.

2 ounces Bacardi light rum
6 ounces (¾ cup) mai tai mix
  (from page 229)
splash Myers's dark rum
splash Bacardi 151 rum

GARNISH
pineapple slice
maraschino cherry
whole lime slice
½ orange slice

1. Fill a 16-ounce glass with ice.
2. Pour light rum and mai tai mix over the ice.
3. Carefully add a splash of Myers's rum and Bacardi 151 to the top of the drink. These are floaters—do not stir.
4. Garnish with a pineapple slice and a cherry slice speared on a paper umbrella. Cut a slit in a whole lime slice and put it on the rim of the glass along with half an orange slice. Serve with a straw.

• MAKES 1 DRINK.

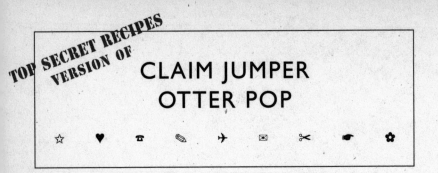

CLAIM JUMPER
OTTER POP

☆ ♥ ☎ ✎ ✈ ✉ ✂ ☛ ✿

Relive the taste of blue Otter Pops with your very first sip from this ingenious concoction. If you ever sucked on an Otter Pop as a kid, you'll have a cool flashback when tasting this one.

1 ounce vodka
½ ounce DeKuyper Wilderberry
    schnapps
½ ounce blue curaçao liqueur
4 ounces (½ cup) sweet & sour
    mix (from page 231)

splash Sprite

GARNISH
lemon slice

1. Fill a 16-ounce glass with ice.
2. Pour all ingredients over ice in the order listed. Do not stir.
3. Cut a slit in a lemon slice and use as a garnish on the rim of the glass. Add a straw and serve.

• MAKES 1 DRINK.

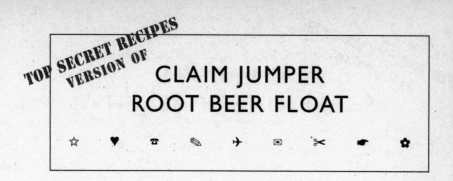

CLAIM JUMPER
ROOT BEER FLOAT

Kahlúa and Galliano combine to duplicate the flavor of a root beer float. You must try it to believe it.

1 ounce Kahlúa liqueur
½ ounce Galliano liqueur

⅓ cup half-and-half
splash Coca-Cola

1. Fill a 14-ounce glass with ice.
2. Add all ingredients in the order listed. Do not stir.
3. Serve with a straw.

• MAKES 1 DRINK.

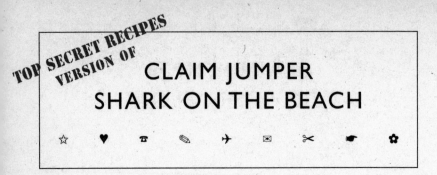

CLAIM JUMPER
SHARK ON THE BEACH

☆ ♥ ☎ ✎ ✈ ✉ ✂ ☞ ✿

The fruity layered drink with a bite. Much better than that other drink "on the beach."

1½ ounces Smirnoff vodka
1 ounce Midori liqueur
1 ounce Chambord liqueur
3 ounces orange juice
3 ounces pineapple juice

splash cranberry juice

GARNISH
pineapple slice
lime slice

1. Fill a 16-ounce glass with ice.
2. Pour all ingredients over ice in the order listed. Do not stir.
3. Cut a slit in a pineapple slice and a lime slice and add the fruit as a garnish to the rim of the glass. Serve with a straw.

• MAKES 1 DRINK.

CLAIM JUMPER TROPICAL STORM

Board up the windows and tie down the patio furniture, then lay the grenadine and passion fruit juice into the bottom of your glass before adding the ice to clone a Tropical Storm. This is how to make a layered drink that absolutely does not suck.

1 ounce passion fruit juice
1 ounce grenadine
1 ounce Malibu rum
1 ounce Myers's dark rum
1 ounce Bacardi light rum
2 ounces (¼ cup) sweet & sour
   mix (from page 231)

2 ounces (¼ cup) orange juice
splash Bacardi 151 rum

GARNISH
orange slice
maraschino cherry

1. Pour the passion fruit juice and grenadine into a 16-ounce glass. Add ice.
2. Pour the rums over the glass in the order listed. Add sweet & sour mix and orange juice. Do not stir.
3. Float a splash of Bacardi 151 over the top of the drink.
4. Garnish with an orange slice and maraschino cherry speared on a toothpick. Serve with a straw.

• MAKES 1 DRINK.

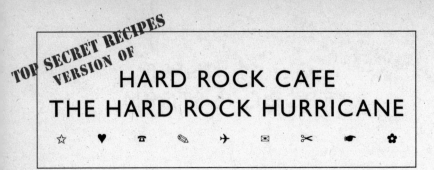

HARD ROCK CAFE
THE HARD ROCK HURRICANE

☆ ♥ ☎ ✎ ✈ ✉ ✂ ☛ ✿

This rock-and-roll theme chain's signature drink comes in a tall souvenir glass that you pay extra for, then take home and never use again. If you don't already have one of the tall glasses covered with dust somewhere in the back of a cupboard, you'll have to find another goblet suitable for 23 ounces of fruity, brain-tingling, theme-chain goodness.

1 ½ ounces Bacardi light rum
6 ounces (¾ cup) mai tai mix
   (from page 229)
¾ ounce Myers's dark rum
¾ ounce amaretto liqueur

GARNISH
lemon wedge
maraschino cherry

1. Fill a 23-ounce glass with ice.
2. Pour all ingredients in the order listed over the ice. Do not stir.
3. Garnish with a lemon wedge and a cherry, and serve with a straw.

• MAKES 1 DRINK.

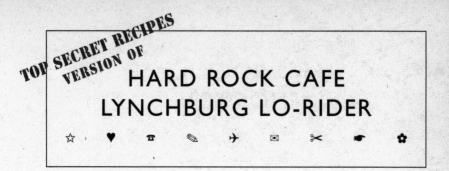

HARD ROCK CAFE
LYNCHBURG LO-RIDER

☆   ♥   ☎   ✑   ✈   ✉   ✂   ☛   ❀

Ever try a Lynchburg lemonade? Good stuff, right? This drink is like one of those, but even better, with the addition of Southern Comfort and a splash of Coke.

¾ ounce Jack Daniel's whiskey
¾ ounce Southern Comfort
½ ounce triple sec liqueur
2 ounces (¼ cup) sweet & sour
   mix (from page 231)

2 ounces (¼ cup) Sprite
splash Coca-Cola

GARNISH
lemon wedge

1. Fill a 12-ounce glass with ice.
2. Pour all ingredients over ice in order listed. Do not stir.
3. Garnish with a lemon wedge and serve with a straw.

• MAKES 1 DRINK.

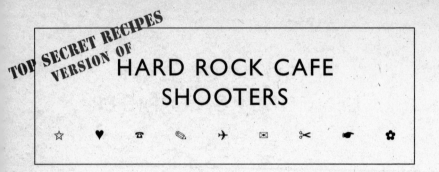

HARD ROCK CAFE
SHOOTERS

☆　♥　☎　✎　✈　✉　✂　☞　✿

When someone at your party yells out that it's time for shooters, you'd better be ready with some good recipes. Here's how the Hard Rock handles a couple of the most popular shooters making the circuit these days. Then turn to pages 200–1 and check out some even more creative and memorable shooter clone recipes from Planet Hollywood that will get your guests grinning.

LEMON DROP

1 ounce Absolut Citron vodka
¾ ounce triple sec liqueur
1 ½ ounces sweet & sour mix
  (from page 231)

juice of 1 lemon wedge
1 teaspoon sugar

1. Combine all ingredients in a shaker with a handful of ice, shake.
2. Strain into a rocks glass and serve.

• MAKES 1 SHOOTER.

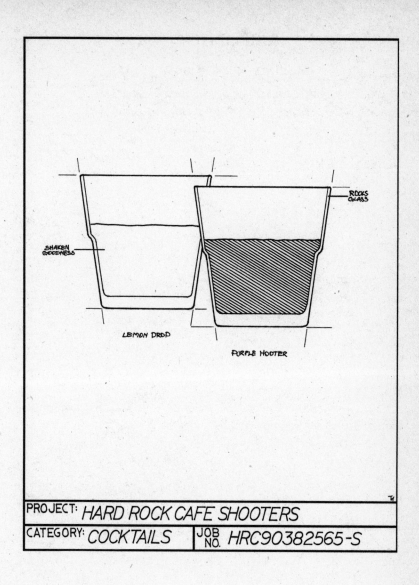

SHAKEN
GOODNESS

ROCKS
GLASS

LEMON DROP

PURPLE HOOTER

PROJECT: *HARD ROCK CAFE SHOOTERS*

CATEGORY: *COCKTAILS* JOB NO. *HRC90382565-S*

PURPLE HOOTER

1 ounce vodka
¾ ounce Chambord liqueur
splash cranberry juice

splash sweet & sour mix
(from page 231)
splash Rose's lime juice
splash Sprite

1. Combine all ingredients in a shaker with a handful of ice, shake.
2. Strain into a rocks glass and serve.

• MAKES 1 SHOOTER.

HOUSE OF BLUES
EVE'S REVENGE MARTINI

☆ ♥ ☎ ✎ ✈ ✉ ✄ ☞ ✿

Sour apple martinis are big-time right now. Every bartender's got a version. Most of the time it's just straight vodka shaken up with sour apple schnapps and ice. With a super-smooth, high-end vodka this is a cherished cocktail. Add a couple other ingredients in there, like sweet & sour mix and lemon-lime soda, and you experience the House of Blues.

1¼ ounces Absolut vodka
¾ ounce DeKuyper Pucker sour
   apple schnapps

1 ounce sweet & sour mix (from
   page 231)
1 ounce Sprite

1. Put a handful of ice in a martini glass so that it chills while you mix.
2. Add another handful of ice to a shaker.
3. Add the vodka, schnapps, sweet & sour mix, and Sprite to the shaker and give it a good shake.
4. Dump the ice out of the martini glass, pour in the cocktail, and serve.

• MAKES 1 DRINK.

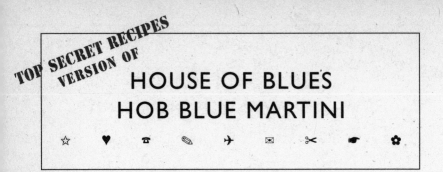

HOUSE OF BLUES
HOB BLUE MARTINI

When making any martini always fill the glass with ice and water and let it sit while you make the drink in a shaker. A glass with a good chill on it is key, whether serving a connoisseur or carefree party animal.

1 ¼ ounces Absolut Citron vodka
¼ ounce blue curaçao liqueur

1 ¼ ounces sweet & sour mix
(from page 231)

1. Put a handful of ice and some water in a martini glass so that it chills while you mix.
2. Add another handful of ice to a shaker.
3. Add the vodka, blue curaçao, and sweet & sour mix to the shaker and give it a good shake.
4. Dump the ice water out of the martini glass, pour in the cocktail, and serve.

• MAKES 1 DRINK.

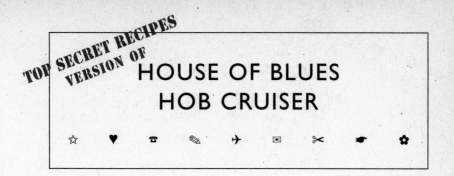

HOUSE OF BLUES
HOB CRUISER

Here's a tasty blue concoction for those who like the sweeter libations, especially the blended kind with tropical flair.

1 cup ice
1 ounce Malibu rum
½ ounce Midori liqueur

½ ounce blue curaçao liqueur
½ cup pina colada mix (from page 230)

1. Combine all ingredients in a blender.
2. Blend on high speed until smooth.
3. Pour into a 12-ounce glass and serve with a straw.

• MAKES 1 DRINK.

HOUSE OF BLUES
MO' BETTA BLUES

☆ ♥ ☎ ✎ ✈ ✉ ✂ ☞ ✿

If you're into trying tasty new margarita variations, you're into this. It's got lemonade in it.

1 ounce Sauza Conmemorativo
   tequila añejo
½ ounce white rum
½ ounce blue curaçao liqueur

2 ounces (¼ cup) lemonade
2 ounces (¼ cup) sweet & sour
   mix (from page 231)

1. Fill a 14-ounce glass with ice.
2. Put all ingredients into a shaker and shake well.
3. Pour the drink over the ice and serve.

• MAKES 1 DRINK.

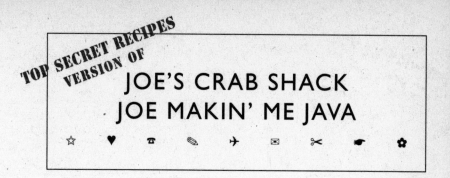

JOE'S CRAB SHACK
JOE MAKIN' ME JAVA

Here's one of Joe's "coffee specialties." It's perfect after your meal, or, for the early crowd, as a morning pick-me-up.

½ ounce Kahlúa liqueur
½ ounce Bailey's Irish Cream

½ ounce amaretto liqueur
1 cup hot coffee

1. Pour Kahlúa, Bailey's, and amaretto into a coffee cup.
2. Add coffee and serve.

• MAKES 1 DRINK.

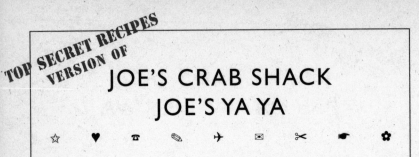

JOE'S CRAB SHACK
JOE'S YA YA

☆　♥　☎　✎　✈　✉　✂　☛　✿

Silly name, delicious drink.

1 ounce vodka
½ ounce peach schnapps
½ ounce Malibu rum
1½ ounces orange juice
1½ ounces pineapple juice
1½ ounces cranberry juice

1 ounce grenadine

GARNISH
orange slice
maraschino cherry

1. Fill a 14-ounce glass with ice.
2. Add all ingredients and shake or stir.
3. Garnish with an orange slice and maraschino cherry on a toothpick. Serve with a straw.

• MAKES 1 DRINK.

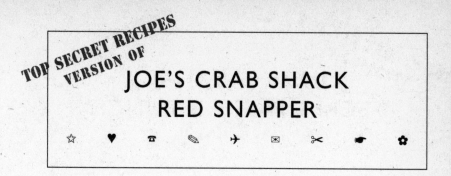

JOE'S CRAB SHACK
RED SNAPPER

☆ ♥ ☎ ✎ ✈ ✉ ✂ ☛ ✿

How about a shooter for whiskey lovers? Whiskey usually isn't my thing, but the amaretto and juice in this one got me all the way through without a shiver.

1 ounce Crown Royal whiskey	2 ounces (¼ cup) cranberry juice
1 ounce amaretto liqueur	

1. Add a handful of ice to a shaker.
2. Add Crown Royal, amaretto, and cranberry juice to shaker, shake thoroughly, and strain into a 6-ounce rocks glass.

• MAKES 1 DRINK.

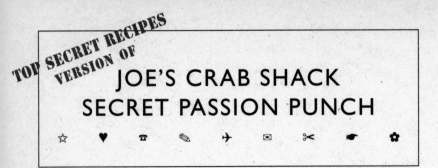

JOE'S CRAB SHACK
SECRET PASSION PUNCH

☆　♥　☎　✏　✈　✉　✂　☞　✿

If you have a choice, use DeKuyper Razzmatazz raspberry schnapps or Hiram Walker Razz Attack for the raspberry liqueur required in this recipe. You'll get a better clone than using Chambord.

1 ounce light rum
½ ounce raspberry liqueur
½ ounce banana liqueur
3 ounces pineapple juice
3 ounces cranberry juice

GARNISH
orange slice
maraschino cherry

1. Fill a 14-ounce glass with ice.
2. Add all ingredients and shake or stir until well blended.
3. Garnish with an orange slice and maraschino cherry on a toothpick. Serve with a straw.

• MAKES 1 DRINK.

JOE'S CRAB SHACK
SHARK TOOTH

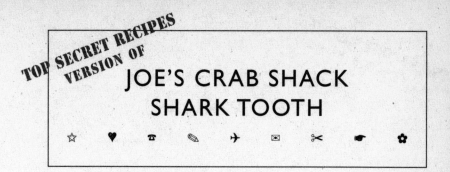

At Joe's they use Whaler's Great White Rum in this drink, but any white rum you have in the cabinet will work fine in this sweet sipper.

1 ounce Whaler's Great White
    Rum
½ ounce Midori liqueur
½ ounce banana liqueur
3 ounces pineapple juice

3 ounces sweet & sour mix (from
    page 231)
½ ounce grenadine

GARNISH
orange slice
maraschino cherry

1. Fill a 16-ounce glass with ice.
2. Add all ingredients, then shake or stir until well blended.
3. Garnish with an orange wedge and maraschino cherry on a toothpick.

• MAKES 1 DRINK.

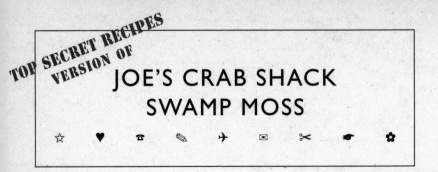

JOE'S CRAB SHACK
SWAMP MOSS

Appropriately named, this green concoction tastes a lot better than it looks.

1 ounce Southern Comfort
½ ounce Midori liqueur
½ ounce Malibu rum
6 ounces pineapple juice

GARNISH
lime wedge

1. Fill a 14-ounce glass with ice.
2. Add all ingredients and shake or stir until well blended.
3. Garnish with a lime wedge and serve with a straw.

• MAKES 1 DRINK.

OLIVE GARDEN CHOCOLATE ALMOND AMORÉ

To make this scrumptious dessert drink the famous Italian chain combines liquid ice cream base with shaved ice to produce a creamy milk shake–like cocktail. We'll just use real ice cream in our secret formula to get this one all up and cloned.

¾ ounce Kahlúa liqueur
¾ ounce Bailey's Irish Cream
¾ ounce amaretto liqueur
¼ teaspoon almond extract
1 scoop vanilla ice cream

6 or 7 ice cubes

GARNISH
Hershey's chocolate syrup
whipped cream

1. Combine all ingredients in a blender and blend on high speed until ice is crushed and drink is smooth.
2. Drizzle chocolate syrup around the inside of a 14-ounce glass.
3. Pour drink into glass, add whipped cream on top, and serve with a straw.

• MAKES 1 DRINK.

OLIVE GARDEN
ITALIAN MARGARITA

This is like a traditional Mexican margarita, except there's a shot of amaretto served on the side for added pleasure. Also, the rim of the glass on the real thing is dipped in green sugar crystals usually used for cake decorating. Looks nice. But it's an optional garnish that's skipped if you don't have any green sugar crystals lying around. And, quite frankly, who does?

1 1/4 ounces Jose Cuervo gold
   tequila
1/2 ounce triple sec liqueur
4 ounces (1/2 cup) sweet & sour
   mix (from page 231)

1 1/4 ounces amaretto liqueur

GARNISH
lime wedge
orange wedge

1. Moisten the rim of a margarita glass and dip it in green sugar crystals.
2. Fill the glass with ice. Add tequila, triple sec, and sweet & sour mix.
3. Serve with a shot of amaretto on the side, and garnish with a lime wedge and orange wedge on the rim.

• MAKES 1 DRINK.

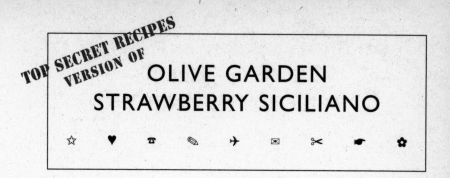

OLIVE GARDEN STRAWBERRY SICILIANO

☆   ♥   ☎   ✎   ✈   ✉   ✂   ☛   ❀

Hop aboard this creamy strawberry shake, 'cause Captain Morgan's at the helm.

1½ ounces Captain Morgan
  spiced rum
1 ounce banana liqueur
¼ cup frozen sweetened sliced
  strawberries, thawed
1 scoop vanilla ice cream

6 to 7 ice cubes

GARNISH
whole strawberry
pineapple slice

1. Combine all ingredients in a blender and blend until ice is crushed and drink is smooth.
2. Pour into a 14-ounce glass and garnish with a whole strawberry and pineapple slice on the rim of the glass. Serve with a straw.

• MAKES 1 DRINK.

OLIVE GARDEN VENETIAN SUNSET

This is a great way to use up the sweet sparkling wine sitting on the shelf, and it's better than a mimosa. Olive Garden uses Martini & Rossi Asti, but you can use whatever you want.

6 ounces (¾ cup) Martini & Rossi
   Asti sparkling wine
3 ounces (approx. ⅓ cup)
   pineapple juice
splash grenadine

GARNISH
pineapple slice
maraschino cherry

1. Fill a 14-ounce glass with ice.
2. Add sparkling wine until the glass is about ⅔ full.
3. Fill to the top with pineapple juice.
4. Add a splash of grenadine, then garnish with a pineapple slice on the rim and drop in a cherry. Serve with a straw.

• MAKES 1 DRINK.

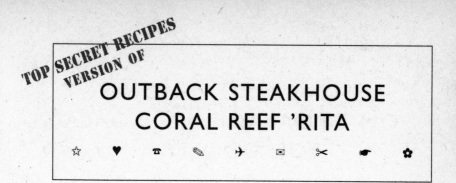

OUTBACK STEAKHOUSE CORAL REEF 'RITA

This Outback margarita selection will handily quench, soothe, and ring the bell in your clock tower. A mildly fruity on-the-rocks margarita is powerful ammunition in any home bartender's arsenal of party cocktails. I like tequila. Tequila is my friend. But get to the bottom of too many of these tasty pink drinks and you'll feel like a used piñata in the morning.

1 ¼ ounces Margaritaville gold tequila
¾ ounce triple sec liqueur
3 ounces (approx. ⅓ cup) sweet & sour mix (from page 231)
3 ounces (approx. ⅓ cup) cranberry juice

¾ ounce Grand Marnier liqueur

GARNISH
wedge of lime

OPTIONAL
margarita salt (for rim of glass)

1. If you want salt on the rim of your glass, moisten the rim of a 16-ounce mug (or glass) and dip it in margarita salt.
2. To make the drink, fill the glass with ice.
3. Add the tequila, triple sec, then some sweet & sour mix and cranberry juice (in equal amounts—about ⅓ cup each should do it) to within a half-inch of the top of the glass. Stir.
4. Splash a half shot of Grand Marnier over the top of the drink.
5. Add a wedge of lime and serve with a straw.

• MAKES 1 DRINK.

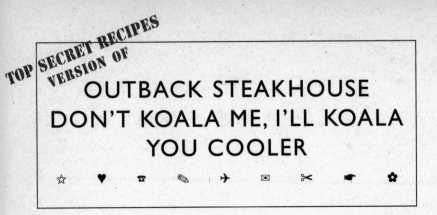

OUTBACK STEAKHOUSE DON'T KOALA ME, I'LL KOALA YOU COOLER

To make this long-winded cocktail clone correctly you must squeeze the juice from a fresh grapefruit. Bottled juice still works, but this cocktail is at its best when you make it the way the big boys do.

1½ ounces vodka
4 ounces (½ cup) fresh squeezed grapefruit juice
2 ounces (¼ cup) sweet & sour mix (from page 231)

splash cranberry juice
splash Sprite

GARNISH
lime wedge

1. Fill a 12-ounce frozen mug (or glass) with ice.
2. Pour all ingredients, except Sprite, over ice.
3. Pour drink into a mixer cup and then back into the mug, to mix.
4. Add a splash of Sprite, and garnish with a lime wedge on the rim. Serve with a straw.

• MAKES 1 DRINK.

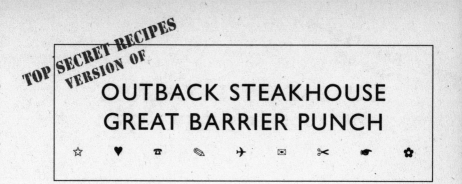

OUTBACK STEAKHOUSE GREAT BARRIER PUNCH

Get out the citrus juicer and start cranking out the o.j. That's what Outback bartenders do, and what you must do as well to become the cocktail clone master.

1½ ounces Malibu rum
¾ ounce Midori liqueur
3 ounces (approx. ⅓ cup) fresh
 squeezed orange juice

3 ounces (approx. ⅓ cup) Ocean
 Spray cranberry juice

GARNISH
orange wedge

1. Fill a 12-ounce frozen mug (or glass) with ice.
2. Pour all ingredients over ice.
3. Pour drink into a mixer cup and then back into the mug, to mix.
4. Garnish with an orange wedge on the rim, and serve with a straw.

• MAKES 1 DRINK.

OUTBACK STEAKHOUSE MELBOURNE COOLER

To juice or not to juice? Sure, you could use a chilled orange juice brand and still make this drink tasty. But if you want big giggles and tips, slap on some elbow grease and juice your own fruit, man. That's how Outback makes this great cocktail, and you, I sense, are no less resourceful. I see it in your eyes.

1 ½ ounces Bacardi Limon rum
2 ounces (¼ cup) sweet & sour
 mix (from page 231)
2 ounces (¼ cup) fresh squeezed
 orange juice

2 ounces (¼ cup) cranberry juice

GARNISH
orange wedge

1. Fill a 12-ounce frozen mug (or glass) with ice.
2. Pour all ingredients over ice.
3. Pour drink into a mixer cup and then back into the mug, to mix.
4. Garnish with an orange wedge on the rim.

- MAKES 1 DRINK.

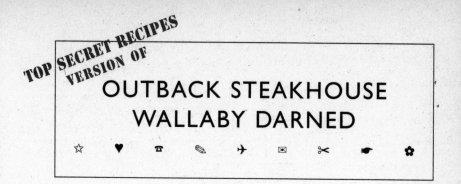

OUTBACK STEAKHOUSE
WALLABY DARNED

The menu describes this steakhouse chain's popular fruity drink as a "down under frozen wonder with peaches, DeKuyper Peachtree schnapps, champagne, Smirnoff vodka, and secret mixers." While you don't need to use the same brand-name booze the chain does, you will need to find a can of Kern's peach nectar to re-create the same secret mixer magic.

1 cup frozen sliced peaches
2 ounces champagne
1 ounce peach schnapps
1 ounce vodka

4 ounces (½ cup) Kern's peach
   nectar
2 or 3 ice cubes

1. Combine all of the ingredients in a blender. Blend on high speed for approximately 30 seconds or until ice is completely crushed and the drink is smooth.
2. Pour into a 12-ounce glass and serve with a straw.

• MAKES 1 DRINK.

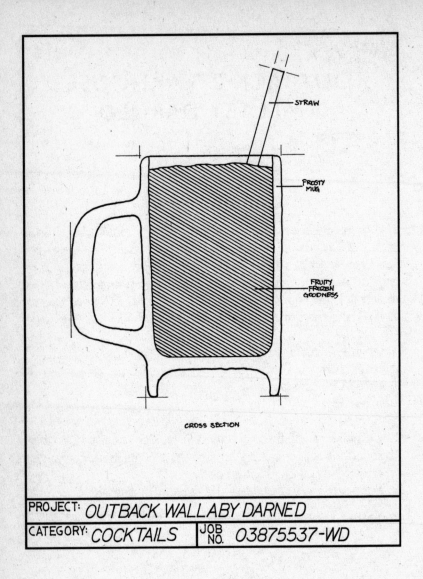

STRAW

FROSTY MUG

FRUITY FROZEN GOODNESS

CROSS SECTION

PROJECT:	*OUTBACK WALLABY DARNED*	
CATEGORY: *COCKTAILS*	JOB NO.	*03875537-WD*

P.F. CHANG'S BUDDHA'S DREAM

☆   ♥   ☎   ✎   ✈   ✉   ✂   ☛   ✿

Even though bartenders are instructed to make this creamy drink without adding ice, go ahead and thicken yours up by adding a few cubes to the blender for more of a shake-like drink with the perfect richness level.

¾ ounce Malibu rum
½ ounce Bacardi light rum
½ ounce Myers's dark rum
¾ ripe banana
4 ounces (½ cup) pineapple juice

1 large scoop vanilla ice cream
dash grenadine

GARNISH
maraschino cherry

1. Combine all ingredients except grenadine in a blender. Blend until smooth.
2. Drizzle grenadine around the inside of a 14-ounce stemmed glass.
3. Pour the drink into the glass, add a maraschino cherry on a toothpick, and serve with a straw.

• MAKES 1 DRINK.

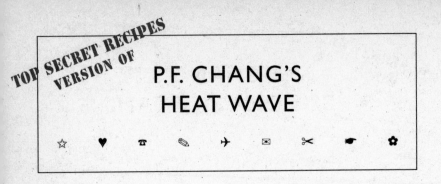

P.F. CHANG'S
HEAT WAVE

Go from zero to hero in seconds with this easy-to-make, and always refreshing, light rum drink.

1¼ ounces Bacardi light rum
1¼ ounces peach schnapps
4 ounces (½ cup) pineapple juice
splash grenadine

GARNISH
pineapple slice
maraschino cherry
paper umbrella

1. Fill a 16-ounce glass with ice.
2. Combine all ingredients in glass over ice. Shake or stir and garnish with a pineapple wedge and maraschino cherry speared on a paper umbrella. Add a straw and serve.

• MAKES 1 DRINK.

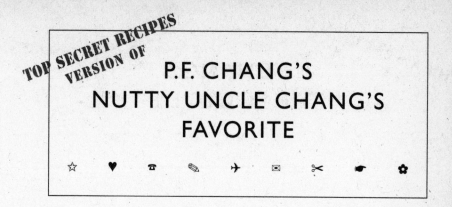

P.F. CHANG'S NUTTY UNCLE CHANG'S FAVORITE

☆ ♥ ☎ ✎ ✈ ✉ ✂ ☞ ✿

You will thaw out a box of frozen strawberries, Grasshopper, to make this most delicious drink in a blender, with rums and juice and amaretto. Ah, yes, you have learned much, my son.

1 ounce Malibu rum
1 ounce Bacardi light rum
½ ounce amaretto liqueur
1½ ounces (3 tablespoons) frozen sweetened sliced strawberries, thawed
2 ounces (¼ cup) pineapple juice

½ cup ice

GARNISH
pineapple slice
maraschino cherry
paper umbrella

1. Combine all ingredients in a blender until ice is crushed.
2. Pour into a 14-ounce stemmed glass. Add a pineapple slice and maraschino cherry speared on a paper umbrella. Serve with a straw.

• MAKES 1 DRINK.

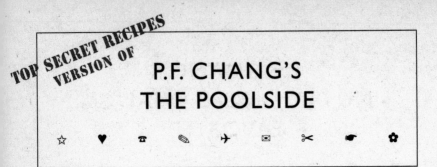

P.F. CHANG'S
THE POOLSIDE

Got pool? Make drink.

1 ¼ ounces Captain Morgan's spiced rum
1 ¼ ounces Malibu rum
2 ounces (¼ cup) orange juice
2 ounces (¼ cup) pineapple juice

splash Sprite

GARNISH
lemon wedge
lime wedge

1. Fill a 16-ounce glass with ice.
2. Combine the rums and juices in the glass, and stir.
3. Add a splash of Sprite, then garnish the drink with a lemon wedge and lime wedge on the rim of the glass. Toss in a straw and serve.

• MAKES 1 DRINK.

PLANET HOLLYWOOD
THE COMET

Arnie, Bruce, Sly, where are you guys going? What's that? To cash in all of your Planet Hollywood stock to buy a dirt bike? Why so gloomy? You still get to share a cool dirt bike. Here, better have a drink. This one's perfect because it's the chain's signature drink and it's really big. It comes in one of those 22-ounce souvenir glasses. You guys probably have a few of those lying around the house, right? Go ask your wives. Oops, sorry, Bruce.

1 ounce vodka
1 ounce Captain Morgan spiced
 rum
1 ounce Myers's rum
3 ounces (approx. ⅓ cup)
 pineapple juice
3 ounces (approx. ⅓ cup) sweet
 & sour mix (from page 231)

3 ounces (approx. ⅓ cup)
 cranberry juice
¾ ounce DeKuyper Razzmatazz
 raspberry schnapps

GARNISH
orange wedge
maraschino cherry

1. Fill a 22-ounce glass with ice.
2. Combine all ingredients, except Razzmatazz, in a shaker and shake well.
3. Pour over ice and add Razzmatazz as a floater to the top of the drink.
4. Garnish with an orange wedge on the rim of the glass, drop in a cherry, add a straw, and serve.

• MAKES 1 DRINK.

PLANET HOLLYWOOD
COOL RUNNING

☆   ♥   ☎   ✎   ✈   ✉   ✂   ☞   ✿

The impressive ingredients list makes for an equally impressive cocktail. Serve this with a 7-dollar cheeseburger, crank up some clips of bad Stallone movies, and it's almost like you're at a famous Hollywood-themed eatery.

¾ ounce Captain Morgan spiced rum
¾ ounce Malibu rum
¾ ounce Bacardi Limon rum
2 ounces (¼ cup) pineapple juice
1 ounce cranberry juice
1 ounce orange juice

splash grenadine
splash Rose's lime juice
splash Bacardi 151 rum

GARNISH
orange wedge
maraschino cherry

1. Fill a 16-ounce glass with ice.
2. Combine all ingredients, except Bacardi 151, in a shaker. Shake, shake, shake.
3. Pour over ice.
4. Pour a splash of Bacardi 151 on top, garnish with an orange wedge on the rim of the glass, drop in a cherry, and serve with a straw.

• MAKES 1 DRINK.

PLANET HOLLYWOOD
MEET JACK BLACK

No, you don't have to love Jack Daniel's to enjoy this drink. But man, it really helps.

1¼ ounces Jack Daniel's whiskey
¾ ounce amaretto liqueur
4 ounces (½ cup) sweet & sour
   mix (from page 231)

splash cola

GARNISH
orange wedge

1. Fill a 16-ounce glass with ice.
2. Combine all ingredients, except cola, in a shaker and shake well.
3. Pour over ice and add a splash of cola.
4. Garnish with an orange wedge, add a straw, and serve.

• MAKES 1 DRINK.

PLANET HOLLYWOOD
SHOOTERS

☆ ♥ ☎ ✎ ✈ ✉ ✂ ☛ ❀

The pressure's on. It's time for shooters and you haven't a clue what to make. Don't worry, I've got your back. Pick any one of these clone recipes for shooters from Planet Hollywood and you'll be tonight's big hero. By the way, it's best to start at the top of the list (Blue Hawaii). See, I told you, I've got your back.

BLUE HAWAII

¾ ounce Malibu Rum
¾ ounce blue curaçao liqueur
splash pineapple juice

splash sweet & sour mix (from
   page 231)

BUBBLE GUM

¾ ounce vodka
¾ ounce banana liqueur

splash cranberry juice
splash grenadine

GRAPE CRUSH

¾ ounce vodka
¾ ounce DeKuyper Pucker Grape
   Liqueur

splash sweet & sour mix (from
   page 231)
splash Chambord liqueur

1. Combine all ingredients for your choice of shooter in a shaker with a handful of ice, and shake.
2. Strain into a 2-ounce shot glass and serve.

• MAKES 1 SHOOTER.

PEANUT BUTTER & JELLY

½ ounce Frangelico liqueur   ½ ounce Bailey's Irish Cream
¾ ounce Chambord liqueur

1. Combine Frangelico and Chambord in a shaker with a handful of ice and shake well.
2. Strain into a 2-ounce shot glass.
3. Gently pour the Bailey's into the shot glass. It will first sink, then rise to the top as a floater.

- MAKES 1 SHOOTER.

PLANET HOLLYWOOD
SWEET DEATH BECOMES HER

☆　♥　☎　✎　✈　✉　✄　☞　✿

With a name like Sweet Death Becomes Her this drink's got to be good. With four different rums in there, you won't care what it's called.

½ ounce light rum
½ ounce Malibu rum
½ ounce Bacardi 151 Rum
½ ounce Captain Morgan spiced
　rum
4 ounces (½ cup) pineapple juice

splash 7UP

GARNISH
pineapple slice
maraschino cherry

1. Fill a 16-ounce glass with ice.
2. Combine all ingredients, except 7UP, in a shaker and shake well.
3. Pour over the ice and add a splash of 7UP on top.
4. Garnish with a pineapple slice on the rim, drop in a maraschino cherry, and serve with a straw.

• MAKES 1 DRINK.

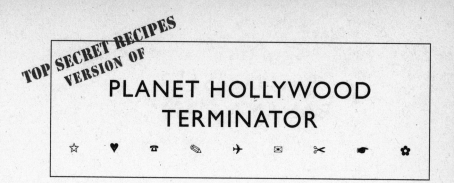

PLANET HOLLYWOOD
TERMINATOR

Terminator is right. Look at all the different liquors that go into this one: vodka, rum, gin, Grand Marnier, Kahlúa. Be sure to paint the ceiling before you start drinking these so that later you'll have something nice to look at.

¾ ounce vodka
¾ ounce white rum
¾ ounce gin
¾ ounce Grand Marnier liqueur
¾ ounce Kahlúa liqueur

2 ounces (¼ cup) sweet & sour
   mix (from page 231)
1 ounce cranberry juice
splash beer

GARNISH
orange wedge

1. Fill a 16-ounce glass with ice.
2. Mix all ingredients, except beer, in a shaker and shake well.
3. Pour over ice.
4. Pour a splash of beer over the top, garnish with an orange wedge, and serve with a straw.

• MAKES 1 DRINK.

RED LOBSTER
BAHAMA MAMA

If you're going to clone a cocktail from Red Lobster you have to include the chain's signature drink, don't you think?

1 ounce Captain Morgan spiced rum

1 ounce Bacardi light rum

3 ounces (approx. ⅓ cup) pineapple juice

3 ounces (approx. ⅓ cup) orange juice

¾ ounce grenadine

1 cup ice

GARNISH
orange wedge

1. Combine all ingredients in a blender. Blend until ice is crushed and drink is smooth.
2. Pour into a 16-ounce glass and garnish with an orange wedge on the rim. Serve with a straw.

• MAKES 1 DRINK.

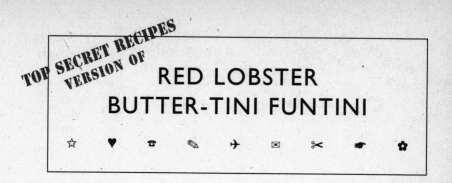

RED LOBSTER
BUTTER-TINI FUNTINI

A creamy white martini that's buttery, rich, and smooth. Plus it's a cinch to make.

1 ½ ounces butterscotch schnapps   *2 ounces (¼ cup) half-and-half*
1 ounce Bailey's Irish Cream

1. Chill a martini glass by filling it with ice and water.
2. Combine all ingredients in a shaker with a handful of ice. Shake well.
3. Dump ice water out of martini glass and pour in drink.

• MAKES 1 DRINK.

RED LOBSTER
THE HAWAIIAN FUNTINI

If it's a "Funtini" is it still a martini? Think about that as you're sipping this simple combination of Malibu rum and homemade pina colada mix served up in a trendy martini glass.

1 ½ ounces Malibu rum
3 ounces (approx. ⅓ cup) pina
   colada mix (from page 230)

1. Chill a martini glass by filling it with ice and water.
2. Combine all ingredients in a shaker with a handful of ice. Shake well.
3. Dump ice water out of martini glass and pour in drink.

- MAKES 1 DRINK.

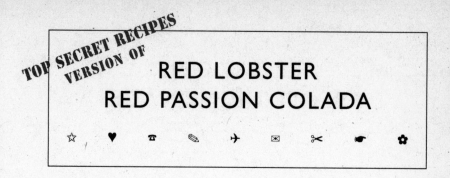

RED LOBSTER
RED PASSION COLADA

Ah, Alizé. The chilled blend of cognac and fruit makes magic with pina colada mix in this take on a chain specialty.

3 ounces Alizé Red Passion
4 ounces (½ cup) pina colada
   mix (from page 230)
1 cup ice

GARNISH
pineapple slice

1. Combine all ingredients in a blender and blend until ice is crushed and drink is smooth.
2. Pour into 14-ounce glass. Add a splash of Alizé to the top of the drink.
3. Garnish with a pineapple slice on the rim of the glass, and serve with a straw.

• MAKES 1 DRINK.

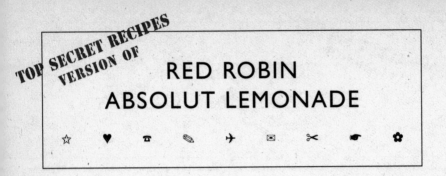

RED ROBIN
ABSOLUT LEMONADE

☆　♥　☏　✎　✈　✉　✂　☞　✿

Amaretto works its nutty magic to set this drink apart from other cloned lemonade cocktails in this book. Use pre-made lemonade or get up the gumption to make it yourself from fresh-squeezed lemons as described in the clone recipes on pages 88–90.

1 ounce Absolut Citron vodka
½ ounce amaretto liqueur
8 ounces (1 cup) lemonade

GARNISH
lemon wedge

1. Fill a 16-ounce glass with ice.
2. Add Absolut Citron and amaretto.
3. Fill with lemonade, add a lemon wedge and a straw, and serve.

• MAKES 1 DRINK.

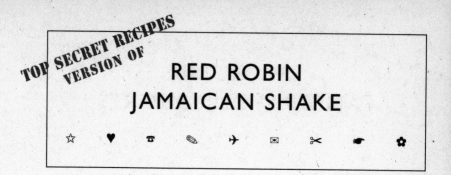

RED ROBIN
JAMAICAN SHAKE

☆ ♥ ☎ ✎ ✈ ✉ ✂ ☞ ✿

More like dessert than a cocktail, really. You won't hear me complain.

½ cup ice
½ ounce amaretto liqueur
½ ounce Grand Marnier liqueur
½ ounce Kahlúa liqueur
2 ounces (¼ cup) milk

1 ½ cups vanilla ice cream

GARNISH
whipped cream

1. Add ½ cup of ice to a blender.
2. Add amaretto, Grand Marnier, Kahlúa, milk, and ice cream to the blender.
3. Blend for 15 to 20 seconds or until the ice is crushed and the drink is smooth.
4. Pour the shake into a large glass, add whipped cream to the top, add a straw, and serve.

• MAKES 1 DRINK.

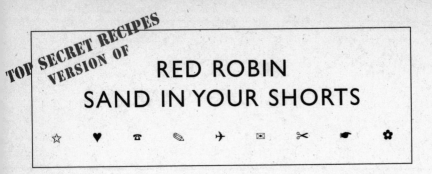

RED ROBIN
SAND IN YOUR SHORTS

To make this layered drink, Chambord is poured into the glass even before the ice is added. Stirring it before serving is not an option.

½ ounce Chambord raspberry
　　liqueur
½ ounce vodka
½ ounce peach schnapps
½ ounce Midori liqueur
½ ounce triple sec liqueur
3 ounces (approx. ⅓ cup) orange
　　juice

1 ounce sweet & sour mix (from
　　page 228)
1 ounce cranberry juice

GARNISH
orange wedge
maraschino cherry

1. Pour the Chambord into the bottom of a 16-ounce glass.
2. Fill the glass with ice, then add the vodka, peach schnapps, Midori, and triple sec.
3. Without stirring the drink, add the orange juice and sweet & sour mix.
4. Top the drink off with the cranberry juice. Serve the drink, unstirred, with a garnish of orange wedge and maraschino cherry speared on a toothpick, plus a straw.

• MAKES 1 DRINK.

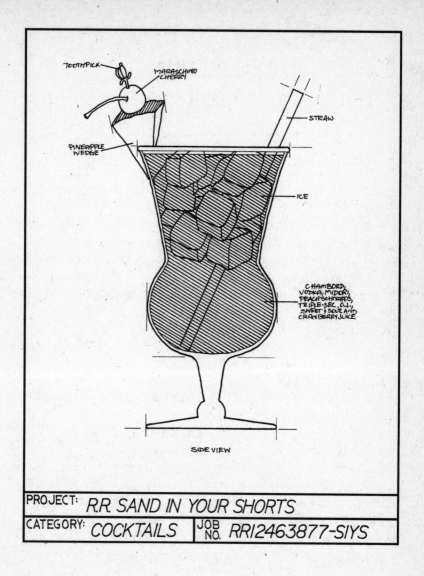

TOOTHPICK

MARASCHINO
CHERRY

STRAW

PINEAPPLE
WEDGE

ICE

CHAMBORD,
VODKA, MIDORI,
PEACH SCHNAPPS,
TRIPLE-SEC, O.J.,
SWEET & SOUR AND
CRANBERRY JUICE

SIDE VIEW

PROJECT: *R.R. SAND IN YOUR SHORTS*

CATEGORY: *COCKTAILS*   JOB NO. *RRI2463877-SIYS*

RED ROBIN
T.N.T.

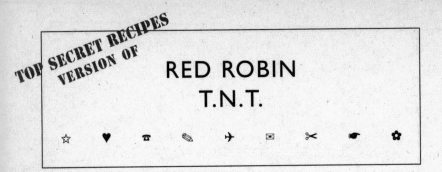

This one's a variation on the old-time potent favorite, Long Island Iced Tea. While the restaurant has another version of this drink made with the less-expensive "well" alcohol, this concoction is whipped up with top shelf stuff comprising—as the menu says— "a powder keg of ingredients ... and a blasting cap full of cola." Still, you can use your favorite liquors or whatever you have on the shelf, be it on the top, middle, or bottom.

½ ounce Beefeater gin
½ ounce Smirnoff vodka
½ ounce Bacardi light rum
½ ounce triple sec liqueur

1 ounce sweet & sour mix (from page 231)
3 to 4 ounces (⅓ to ½ cup) cola

GARNISH
lemon wedge

1. Add ice to a 16-ounce glass.
2. Add the ingredients in the order listed, topping the drink off with Pepsi or Coke to the top of the glass.
3. Add a wedge of lemon and a straw, and serve.

• MAKES 1 DRINK.

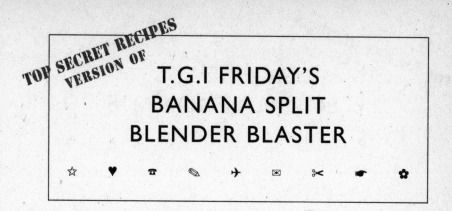

T.G.I FRIDAY'S BANANA SPLIT BLENDER BLASTER

If you ever crave a banana split, but don't have all the ingredients, mosey over to your well-stocked bar and make one of these drinks from Friday's Blender Blaster selections. It's like drinking the traditional version you usually consume with a spoon.

½ ounce banana liqueur
½ ounce strawberry liqueur
½ ounce crème de cacao liqueur
2 scoops vanilla ice cream
2 ounces (¼ cup) frozen
  sweetened sliced strawberries,
  thawed
½ ripe banana

3 ounces (approx. ⅓ cup) milk
½ cup ice

GARNISH
whipped cream
banana slice
maraschino cherry

1. Put all ingredients in a blender and blend on high speed until smooth. You may have to stop the blender to stir the drink with a spoon to help it blend better.
2. Pour drink into a 14-ounce glass. Add a dollop of whipped cream on top of the drink, then add a banana slice to the edge of the glass.
3. Put a maraschino cherry on the side of the whipped cream and serve with a straw.

• MAKES 1 DRINK.

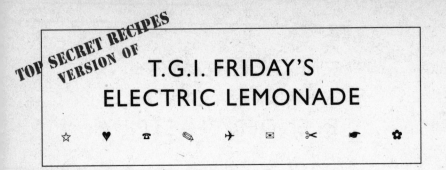

T.G.I. FRIDAY'S
ELECTRIC LEMONADE

Good thing you're wearing aqua blue so this drink won't show up when Dexter over there spills one on you. Fortunately, or unfortunately, this version of Friday's bright blue lemonade cocktail goes down real fast, be it into your gullet or onto a cosmic jumpsuit.

1 ¼ ounces vodka
1 ounce blue curaçao liqueur
4 ounces (½ cup) sweet & sour
    mix (from page 231)

splash Sprite

GARNISH
lemon wedge

1. Fill 14-ounce glass with ice.
2. Add vodka, blue curaçao, and sweet & sour mix to a shaker and shake it up.
3. Pour the drink over the ice, add a splash of Sprite followed by a squeezed lemon wedge and a straw.

• MAKES 1 DRINK.

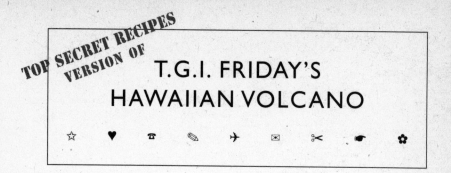

T.G.I. FRIDAY'S
HAWAIIAN VOLCANO

Behold, the eruption of sweet, fruity flavors. Okay, that was bad. But the drink's great.

1 ounce vodka
1 ounce amaretto liqueur
¾ ounce Southern Comfort
2 ounces (¼ cup) pineapple juice
2 ounces (¼ cup) orange juice
½ ounce lime juice
¾ ounce grenadine

GARNISH
orange slice
lemon wedge
lime wedge
maraschino cherry

1. Fill a 14-ounce glass with ice.
2. Shake up all liquid ingredients in a shaker. Pour over the ice.
3. Add an orange slice to the rim of the glass, then add a wedge of lemon and a wedge of lime into the glass. Finish it off with a maraschino cherry and a straw.

• MAKES 1 DRINK.

T.G.I. FRIDAY'S
JUNE BUG

I know candy. I like candy. And this drink, senator, tastes just like candy.

1 ounce Midori liqueur
¾ ounce Malibu rum
¾ ounce banana liqueur
2 ounces (¼ cup) pineapple juice

2 ounces (¼ cup) sweet & sour
  mix (from page 231)

GARNISH
maraschino cherry

1. Fill a 14-ounce glass with ice.
2. Shake all liquid ingredients in a shaker and pour over the ice.
3. Add a maraschino cherry and a straw.

• MAKES 1 DRINK.

T.G.I. FRIDAY'S
LIGHTS OF HAVANA

☆   ♥   ☎   ✎   ✈   ✉   ✄   ☞   ✿

Just because it's tropical doesn't mean it's typical. There's a lot of Malibu rum flowing out there these days, and when it's mixed with Midori and fruit juices you've got a drink only those without a single sweet tooth in them could turn down.

1 ¼ ounces Malibu rum
1 ¼ ounces Midori liqueur
2 ounces (¼ cup) orange juice
2 ounces (¼ cup) pineapple juice
splash soda

GARNISH
orange slice
lime slice

1. Fill a 14-ounce glass with ice.
2. Add liquid ingredients to a shaker and shake well. Pour over ice.
3. Cut a bit into a slice of orange and a slice of lime and add them to the rim of the glass. Throw in a straw and serve.

• MAKES 1 DRINK.

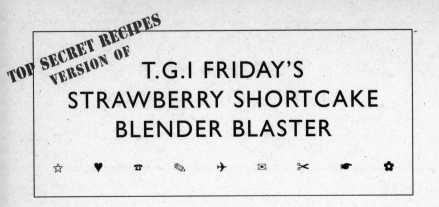

T.G.I FRIDAY'S STRAWBERRY SHORTCAKE BLENDER BLASTER

☆   ♥   ☎   ✎   ✈   ✉   ✂   ☛   ✿

Friday's gave its selection of ice cream cocktails the spiffy name "Blender Blasters," otherwise known as milk shakes with an attitude. Shock 'em all with this one when amaretto pitches in to help re-create the taste of a real strawberry shortcake.

1 ½ ounces amaretto liqueur
2 scoops vanilla ice cream
2 ounces (¼ cup) milk
2 ounces (¼ cup) frozen
   sweetened sliced strawberries,
   thawed

½ cup ice

GARNISH
whipped cream
1 fresh strawberry

1. Put all ingredients in a blender and blend on high speed until smooth. You may have to stop the blender to stir the drink with a spoon to help it blend better.
2. Pour drink into a 14-ounce glass. Add a dollop of whipped cream on top of the drink, then add a fresh strawberry to the edge of the glass. Serve with a straw.

• MAKES 1 DRINK.

Z'TEJAS
Z' BIG STICK MARGARITA

☆　♥　☎　✎　✈　✉　✂　☛　✿

In the southwestern cities where Z'Tejas serves these incredible margaritas, they are truly legendary. The secret mixture is made fresh every day in a freezing dispenser machine with a dirt-cheap brand of tequila and custom-made sweet & sour mix. Perhaps that's the beauty of this drink. It's one of the most potent margaritas around, but with the addition of sweet liqueurs, its strength is well hidden. Even though the chain uses a special machine to make this one, preparing your own clone doesn't require any special equipment. It does take patience, however. Most good things do. But before long you'll be enjoying either a clone of Z' Big Stick with three layers of liqueurs, or a copy of the Famous Chambord Raspberry Margarita, the drink that earns "Best Margarita in Town" awards for the chain on a regular basis. That recipe follows this one.

You can, of course, drink the basic margarita base without the liqueurs, but the added liqueurs give the drink its charm. To create the margarita, you just mix all the ingredients in a pitcher and put it in the freezer for at least 4 hours, even overnight if you can. The cocktail won't freeze solid since there's tequila in there. When it's frozen, you take it out, and give it a little stir until it's the perfect slushy consistency.

This recipe clones the tall, 14-ounce drink served in a pilsner glass with layers of Chambord, Midori, and blue curaçao. The restaurant limits customers to just two of these drinks per visit. Try it and you'll find out why.

2 cups warm water
½ cup granulated sugar
⅓ cup fresh lime juice
⅓ cup fresh lemon juice
5 ounces Montezuma gold tequila
2½ ounces triple sec liqueur

1 ounce Midori liqueur
1 ounce Chambord liqueur
1 ounce blue curaçao liqueur

GARNISH
2 lime wedges

1. Combine sugar with warm water in a pitcher and stir or shake until sugar is dissolved. Add lime juice, lemon juice, tequila, and triple sec and put pitcher in the freezer for several hours, until drink is frozen.
2. When drink is frozen, use a long spoon to mix up the drink so that it is slushy and smooth. The alcohol in the drink will prevent it from freezing solid so that you can easily break it up by stirring.
3. To make the drink, pour ½ ounce of Midori into the bottom of 2 14-ounce pilsner glasses. Add about ¼ cup of the frozen margarita on top of the liqueur. Pour ½ ounce of Chambord into each glass, then add another ¼ cup of frozen margarita. Add ½ ounce blue curaçao to each glass and top off the drink with the remaining frozen margarita.
4. Add a straw and lime wedge to each drink and serve.

• MAKES 2 14-OUNCE DRINKS.

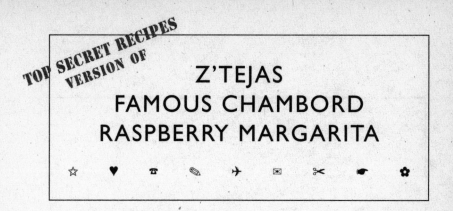

Z'TEJAS FAMOUS CHAMBORD RASPBERRY MARGARITA

At only 10½ ounces per serving you might think this drink a bit wee. But I assure you, just one of these packs a wallop, and two will get you speaking in haiku. This delicious raspberry margarita, along with an incredible southwestern cuisine, is making this small chain a growing success story.

2 cups warm water
½ cup granulated sugar
⅓ cup fresh lime juice
⅓ cup fresh lemon juice
5 ounces Montezuma gold tequila
2½ ounces triple sec liqueur

1½ ounces Chambord raspberry liqueur

GARNISH
3 lime wedges

1. Combine sugar with warm water in a pitcher and stir or shake until sugar is dissolved. Add lime juice, lemon juice, tequila, and triple sec and put the pitcher in the freezer for several hours, until the drink is frozen. This is the straight margarita.
2. When drink is frozen, use a long spoon to mix it up so it's slushy and smooth. The alcohol in the drink will prevent it from freezing solid so that you can easily break it up by stirring.
3. To make each drink, pour ½ ounce of Chambord into the bottom of 3 10½-ounce glasses—large martini glasses work well for this. Pour the frozen margarita over the liqueur and it will swirl itself into the drink.

4. Add a straw to each drink plus a lime wedge and serve.

• MAKES 3 10.5-OUNCE DRINKS.

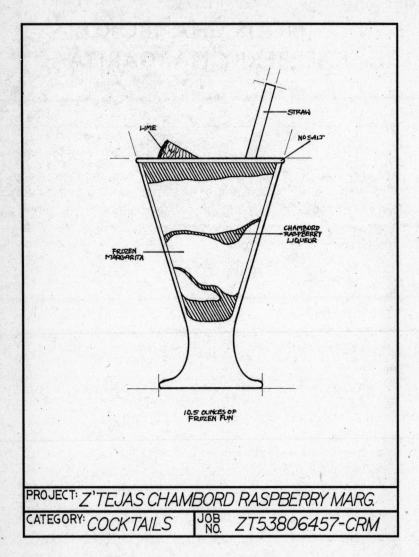

STRAW

LIME

NO SALT

CHAMBORD
RASPBERRY
LIQUEUR

FROZEN
MARGARITA

10.5 OUNCES OF
FROZEN FUN

PROJECT: Z'TEJAS CHAMBORD RASPBERRY MARG.

CATEGORY: COCKTAILS   JOB NO. ZT53806457-CRM

SPIRITS:

MIXERS

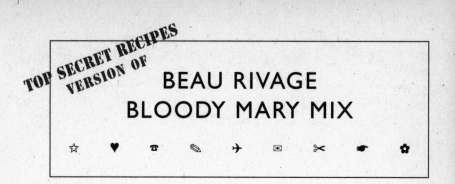

BEAU RIVAGE
BLOODY MARY MIX

☆ ♥ ☎ ✎ ✈ ✉ ✂ ☛ ✿

Why make a clone recipe for an obscure bloody mary mix from a Biloxi, Mississippi, casino? Because I've had every major bloody mary mix brand on the market and none can compare to this one. With other mixes I find myself doctoring up the drink with additional Tabasco or salt or Worcestershire sauce. That's sure not the case here. This mix tastes great right out of the bottle, and it doesn't even contain horseradish, which is commonly found in good bloody marys. Make this one soon and keep it handy.

1 6-ounce can tomato paste
2 cups water
1 12-ounce can V-8 vegetable
   juice
⅓ cup distilled white vinegar
¼ cup Worcestershire sauce

2 teaspoons Lawry's seasoned
   salt
1¼ teaspoons ground black
   pepper
½ teaspoon Tabasco

Combine all ingredients in a pitcher and stir well. Combine with vodka to make bloody mary cocktails.

• MAKES 1 QUART.

MARA
SIMPLE SYRUP

Simple syrup will sometimes be needed to mix great-tasting drinks that require additional sweetening. Use enough of the clone recipes for cocktails in this book and you'll eventually need to use some simple syrup.

½ cup hot water
½ cup sugar

Stir ingredients together until sugar is dissolved.

• MAKES APPROX. 7 OUNCES.

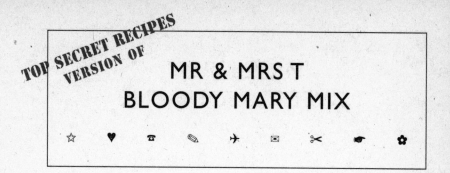

MR & MRS T BLOODY MARY MIX

Here's a way to clone the famous and very popular bloody mary mix from that couple with a letter for a last name. It's a simple-to-make blend of tomato juice and spices with some prepared horseradish and canned jalapeño juice thrown in for a "spicier, zestier" drink. Mix this with vodka over ice and you've got a delicious cocktail. But if you're not in the mood to get zoinked, this clone recipe is also a great way to kick up your tomato juice, just for drinking straight.

1 46-ounce can tomato juice
4 tablespoons lime juice
3 tablespoons juice from canned
   jalapeños (nacho slices)
3 tablespoons vinegar
2 tablespoons sugar

2 teaspoons prepared horseradish
¼ teaspoon salt
¼ teaspoon pepper
⅛ teaspoon onion powder
dash garlic

1. Combine all ingredients in a 2-quart pitcher. Store covered in the refrigerator.
2. Directions for mixing a drink, as per the original mix: "Add 3 parts Mr & Mrs T Rich & Spicy Bloody Mary Mix to 1 part vodka, gin, rum or tequila, over ice. Mr & Mrs T Rich & Spicy Bloody Mary Mix is also delicious by itself. Simply pour over ice and serve."

• MAKES 52 OUNCES.

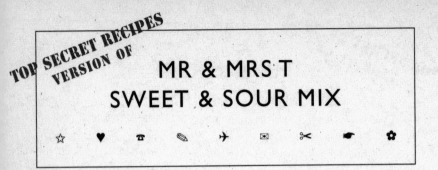

MR & MRS T
SWEET & SOUR MIX

☆ ♥ ☎ ✎ ✈ ✉ ✂ ☞ ✿

This clone recipe makes a little more of the popular sweet & sour mixer than you'll get in the 34-ounce plastic bottles at the store. So now when you crave that frosty margarita or snappy whiskey sour and don't have any sweet & sour mix on hand, you can whip together a batch of your own. Just mix this stuff, as you would the brand-name sweet & sour mix, in your favorite cocktails and party libations.

3 cups hot water
¾ cup bottled lime juice
½ cup corn syrup

¼ cup granulated sugar
¼ cup bottled lemon juice
1 drop yellow food coloring

Combine all ingredients in a 2-quart pitcher and mix until sugar is dissolved. Store covered in refrigerator.

• MAKES 40 OUNCES.

RESTAURANT-STYLE MAI TAI MIX

Use this in restaurant drink clones that require fresh mai tai mix. To make it you'll need passion fruit nectar, which can be hard to find in some stores. In that case use passion fruit juice that's blended with another juice, such as Mauna Lai Paradise Passion guava/passion fruit blend.

¼ cup orange juice
¼ cup pineapple juice
¼ cup passion fruit juice

2 tablespoons maraschino cherry juice
1½ tablespoons simple syrup (from page 226)

Combine ingredients in a pitcher. Cover and refrigerate until needed.

• MAKES APPROX. 1 CUP.

RESTAURANT-STYLE
PINA COLADA MIX

☆　♥　☎　✎　✈　✉　✂　☞　✿

Use this in restaurant drink clones that require fresh pina colada mix. This tastes exactly five-and-a-half times better than any pina colada mix you get out of a bottle.

1 1/3 cups cream of coconut　　　　3 1/2 cups pineapple juice
　(one 15-ounce can)

Combine ingredients in a pitcher. Cover and refrigerate until needed.

• MAKES APPROX. 4¾ CUPS.

RESTAURANT-STYLE
SWEET & SOUR MIX

This is a versatile, fresh recipe for restaurant drinks that require sweet & sour mix. It's so good you'll want to drink it straight.

1 cup hot water
¼ cup granulated sugar
3 tablespoons fresh lime juice

3 tablespoons fresh lemon juice
1 drop yellow food coloring

1. Combine the hot water with the sugar and stir until sugar dissolves.
2. Add lime juice and lemon juice and food coloring. Chill.

• MAKES 1½ CUPS.

TRADEMARKS

A&W, Dr Pepper, 7UP, Squirt, and Hawaiian Punch are registered trademarks of Dr Pepper/Seven Up, Inc.

Coca-Cola, Fresca, and Minute Maid are registered trademarks of The Coca-Cola Company

Slice is a registered trademark of Pepsi-Cola Company

Sonic Drive-In and Ocean Water are registered trademarks of America's Drive-In Trust

T.G.I. Friday's and Flings are registered trademarks of TGI Friday's, Inc.

Applebee's is a registered trademark of Applebee's International, Inc.

Baskin-Robbins and BR Blast are registered trademarks of Baskin-Robbins, Inc.

Jamba Juice is a registered trademark of Jamba Juice Company

Orange Julius, Dairy Queen, and Blizzard are registered trademarks of American Dairy Queen Corp.

Red Robin is a registered trademark of Red Robin Gourmet Burgers, Inc.

Starbucks, Tazoberry, Tazo, and Frappuccino are registered trademarks of Starbucks Corporation

Arby's is a registered trademark of Arby's, Inc.

Cinnabon, Icescape, and Mochalatta Chill are registered trademarks of AFC Enterprises

Baby Ruth, Butterfinger, and Nestea are registered trademarks of Nestlé USA

Jack in the Box is a registered trademark of Jack in the Box, Inc.

Oreo and General Foods International Coffees are registered trademarks of Kraft Foods, Inc.

McDonald's, McFlurry, and Shamrock Shake are registered trademarks of McDonald's Corporation

M&M's is a registered trademark of Mars, Inc.

BIBLIOGRAPHY

Broom, David. *Spirits & Cocktails*. London: Carlton Books, 1998.

Cresswell, Stephen. *Homemade Root Beer, Soda & Pop*. Pownal, VT: Storey Communications, 1998.

Herbst, Sharon Tyler. *Food Lover's Companion*. Hauppauge, NY: Barron's Educational Series, Inc., 1990.

Pendergrast, Mark. *For God, Country and Coca-Cola*. New York, NY: Collier Books, 1993.

Witzel, Michael Karl & Young-Witzel, Gyvel. *Soda Pop!* Stillwater, MN: Voyageur Press, Inc., 1998

World Book, Inc. *The World Book Encyclopedia*. Chicago, IL: World Book, Inc., 1986.

Wyman, Carolyn. *I'm a Spam Fan*. Stamford, CT: Longmeadow Press, 1993.

INDEX

More Top Secret Recipes from
TODD WILBUR